D1625241

THE BEST
ADVICE EVER

FOR

Teachers

THE BEST ADVICE EVER

FOR

Teachers

CHARLES MCGUIRE
AND DIANA ABITZ
EDITED BY PATRICK DOBSON

**Andrews McMeel
Publishing**

Kansas City

01 02 03 04 05 QUF 10 9 8 7 6 5 4 3 2 1

Library of Congress Cataloging-in-Publication Data

McGuire, Charles.
    The best advice ever for teachers / [compiled by] Charles McGuire and Diana Abitz ; edited by Patrick Dobson.
        p. cm.
    ISBN 0-7407-1011-7
    1. Teachers—Quotations. 2. Teaching—Quotations, maxims, etc. I. Abitz, Diana. II. Dobson, Patrick. III. Title.
    LB1775 .M315 2001
    371.1—dc21

                                        2001020426

*This book is dedicated to
our contributors and to educators
who have shape our lives and minds
with their wisdom, counsel, and concern,
especially to those whose passion for teaching
has encouraged us to be life-long learners.
We also dedicate this book to our children,
Jenny, Austin, Maggie, Johnny, and Callie,
whose lives are touched each day by thoughtful,
encouraging, and inspiring teachers.*

CONTENTS

Foreword ... ix
Acknowledgments ... xi

They really make lives happen.
They do. I love teachers.

—AL PACINO, ON RECEIVING THE CECIL B. DEMILLE LIFETIME
ACHIEVEMENT GOLDEN GLOBE AWARD (2001)

Pacino attributed much of his success in films to his high school drama teacher. And like Pacino, we all have a story of a teacher. It could be the college professor who opened up a world of wonder in a profession or field of study we never dreamed of before. Or the high school or grade school teacher who fired an interest in a career that never ceased.

Teaching is at once a vastly important and underrated profession. Despite low pay and constant criticism, teachers tend our most precious asset as a society and civilization—the minds of students. They try, against all obstacles, to pass on the accumulated knowledge, energy, and creativity of our culture. Often, they achieve wild success despite the difficulties.

Only gifted and dedicated people last in a profession whose constant is change. Teachers must not only perform and achieve according to standards, but they must also become babysitters, caregivers, nurses, and sometimes transportation services. These added responsibilities demand tremendous energy, patience, and fortitude—not to mention an interest in the profession and need to train and retrain.

This is a book that will give successful teachers perspective. The experts, educators, professionals, and coaches speaking here will inspire teachers to even greater success—for themselves and their charges.

This is also a book for difficult times. The demands of the profession will give most teachers pause. Doubt is a constant companion, and staying motivated is sometimes difficult. The words here serve to remind teachers that even in the darkest moments, a bit of humor, a change of attitude, and a motivational or inspirational word of advice to students can help to turn a day, a quarter, or semester around.

—Patrick Dobson, editor

ACKNOWLEDGMENTS

The authors would like to acknowledge winners of the Milken National Education Award for their role in making this book possible, and the principles of the Teel Institute, whose comments and observations contributed significantly to the content. We would also like to thank Allan Stark and Patrick Dobson of Stark Books (Andrews McMeel Publishing) for their support, guidance, and confidence in this project.

CHAPTER 1

Spirit of the Teacher

A teacher who is attempting to teach without inspiring the pupil with a desire to learn is hammering on cold iron.

—HORACE MANN (1796–1859), AMERICAN EDUCATOR WHO ESTABLISHED THE MASSACHUSETTS STATE BOARD OF EDUCATION

Through the ages, teachers have helped to shape and mold the minds of students. There seem to be certain characteristics common to all educators, who have mastered the ability to impart and convey the wisdom of the ages. Combined, those attributes are the spirit of the teacher.

Teachers who take their profession seriously and make subjects come alive are the ones who leave an unforgettable and indelible mark on the student. They impart a way of life. They wear their subject like a favorite coat or sweater. By doing so, the student sees a life lived with purpose, meaning, and passion. When the spirit of the teacher connects with the spirit of the student, the best of the student surfaces and thrives.

When I was in eighth grade, my American history teacher, Mrs. Deets, was so excited by the subject that hardly anyone left her classroom not similarly excited. Her love of our country's history was evident in the classroom every day. She loved to teach about the Federalist Papers and the division between those who wanted states' rights and those who wanted a centralized government. It was pretty heady stuff in eighth grade, but it was her passion for the subject that made an impression on me.

—CHERYL BLANCHARD, HIGH SCHOOL
HISTORY TEACHER, CHICAGO, ILLINOIS

An understanding heart is everything in a teacher, and cannot be esteemed highly enough. One looks back with appreciation to the brilliant teachers, but with gratitude to those who touched our human feeling. The curriculum is so much necessary raw material, but warmth is the vital element for the growing plant and for the soul of the child.

—CARL JUNG (1875–1961), SWISS PSYCHOLOGIST
AND CONTEMPORARY OF SIGMUND FREUD

The human spirit is your specifically human dimension and contains abilities other creatures may not have. Every human is spiritual; in fact, spirit is the essence of being human. You have a body that may become ill; you have a psyche that may become disturbed. But the spirit is what you are. It is your healthy core.

—JOSEPH FABRY (1909–1999),
AMERICAN WRITER AND PSYCHOLOGIST

Sincerity, or trustworthiness, or the gift of inspiring confidence, should be an intrinsic quality in a teacher. He starts with a great advantage over his students—he is older, more experienced, and therefore presumably wiser than they, and they realize it. If they are certain that his motives are honest and that he is trying his level best, they can overlook his mistakes, provided he does not make too may of them.

—CLAUDE M. FUESS, *CREED OF A SCHOOL-MASTER* (1939)

People expect teachers to teach. They value lucid exposition, the clear statement of problems and guidance to their solution. Personal qualities of kindness, sympathy, and patience are secondary, appreciated by pupils if they make the teacher more effective in carrying out his primary intellectual task.

—FRANK MUSGROVE AND PHILIP TAYLOR,
SOCIETY AND THE TEACHER'S ROLE (1969)

Good teaching is one-fourth preparation and three-fourths theatre.

—GAIL GODWIN, *THE ODD WOMEN* (1974)

The professor's journey is one that goes to the edge of the known world. One of the aims of the journey is to push back the boundaries of that world and to discover ways of engaging others in this task and of sharing with them all its mystery and wonder.

—CRAIG KRIDEL, ROBERT V. BULLOUGH, JR., AND PAUL SHAKER,
TEACHERS AND MENTORS (1996)

Greatness, whether in the classroom or in day-to-day living, is intentional. Success doesn't come at once, but over a lifetime. The outstanding teacher is aware of the little things in her students' lives. She recognizes a spark of inspiration and nurtures it to a flaming passion for learning.

—JOANNE FEIST, RETIRED TEACHER, OAKLAND, CALIFORNIA

I set high standards for my students and offer many personal conferences and individual suggestions for ways that they can attain these standards. I see part of my job as a teacher to stretch students—to encourage them to excellent work and to progress to higher levels of thinking, reading, and writing. I try to show them that learning is both lifelong and fun. I praise them when their work or progress deserves praise, though sometimes I have to look very hard to find things to praise.

—DR. GLORIA HENDERSON, PROFESSOR OF HUMANITIES, GORDON COLLEGE, BARNESVILLE, GEORGIA

When I was in sixth grade my mother died. Mrs. Gladney, my teacher, sensing the sorrow and helplessness I felt, became a great encourager to me. She'd have me do special projects in the class—sometimes by myself and at other times with fellow students. Even though she never talked to me at length about my mom's death, I knew she was concerned. One time, she asked me to go with her outside to collect leaves from the variety of trees that surrounded the school grounds. We walked for almost an hour and collected all different kinds of leaves. After having explained the difference to me, she looked at me and told me how proud my

4

mother would be with the way I carried on after her passing. In her many quiet ways, Mrs. Gladney helped me live through a very difficult time in my life.

—SHANNON WILSON, RETIRED HIGH SCHOOL
TEACHER, KNOXVILLE, TENNESSEE

The teacher must derive not only the capacity, but also the desire, to observe natural phenomena. The teacher must understand and feel her position of observer: The activity must lie in the phenomenon. We teachers can only help the work going on, as servants wait upon a master.

—MARIA MONTESSORI (1870–1952),
ITALIAN EARLY CHILDHOOD EDUCATOR

The first duty of love is to listen.

—PAUL TILLICH (1886–1965), PROFESSOR
OF THEOLOGY, UNIVERSITY OF CHICAGO

People who listen always learn more and generally know more. That was one of the lessons I learned very early on from a professor of education. He told us that mastering the contents of the subject matter was only half the job. The other half was listening to what it was telling us. The same is true with students. Listening just to their words hardly qualifies for good listening. Hearing what they say is a whole lot different than hearing them say it.

—BETH JOHNSTON, EIGHTH-GRADE SCIENCE
TEACHER, WASHINGTON, D.C.

So when you are listening to somebody, completely, attentively, then you are listening not only to the words, but also to the feeling of what is being conveyed, to the whole of it, not part of it.

—J. KRISHNAMURTI (1895–1986),
EAST INDIAN PHILOSOPHER AND WRITER

Empathic listening is so powerful because it gives you accurate data to work with. Instead of projecting your own autobiography and assuming thoughts, feelings, motives, and interpretation, you're dealing with the reality inside another person's head and heart. You're listening to understand. You're focused on receiving the deep communication of another human soul.

—STEPHEN COVEY, *THE SEVEN HABITS OF
HIGHLY EFFECTIVE PEOPLE* (1989)

Humor must professedly teach and it must not professedly preach, but it must do both if it would live forever.

—MARK TWAIN (1835–1910)

Among those whom I like or admire, I can find no common denominator, but among those with whom I love, I can: All of them make me laugh.

—W. H. AUDEN (1907–1973), ENGLISH POET AND TEACHER

How anyone can teach without a sense of humor is beyond me. I don't know a teacher who doesn't have the ability to laugh at themselves and the sometimes silly situations that occur in the classroom. I'm not talking about the giggling kind of humor, but the kind that shows us our humanity. Too often we take ourselves too seriously. When the kids make mistakes after working hard on a given project, I try to help them see the positive side of things. Often that means laughing at us.

—HELEN GURSKI, NINTH-GRADE GEOGRAPHY TEACHER,
LOS ANGELES, CALIFORNIA

Orientation towards others is essential. The effective teacher has a deep and genuine respect for, and understanding of, others as persons . . . His insight into human dignity enables him to work for and with others for what is best for them . . .

His sense of security contributes greatly to the kind of person he is. Personal security gives him a tolerance for "humanness," the needed flexibility and adaptability that enables him to meet change, and the important sense of humor that permits him to laugh with others—and, at times, himself.

—JAMES M. CRONIN, "IMPROVING YOUR CLASSROOM PRODUCTIVITY,"
IN *PRENTICE-HALL TEACHERS ENCYCLOPEDIA* (1970)

Having a sense of humor shows the students that you're human. I think being able to show a sense of humor can diffuse the tensions that sometimes arise in the classroom. I once assigned a chapter from *To Kill a Mockingbird* to my class for review the following week. When it came time to review it, I began with an introduction where I tried sounding like one of the main characters, Atticus Finch. My class looked at me dumbfounded and then starting laughing. I laughed too when I realized that that week's review was to be on John Steinbeck's *Of Mice and Men*!

—JAMES BUCHANAN, TENTH-GRADE ENGLISH TEACHER,
PHILADELPHIA, PENNSYLVANIA

Some men give up their designs when they have almost reached the goal; while others, on the contrary, obtain a victory by exerting, at the last moment, more vigorous efforts than ever before.

—HERODOTUS (484?–425? B.C.), GREEK PHILOSOPHER
KNOWN AS THE "FATHER OF HISTORY"

Permanence, perseverance, and persistence in spite of all obstacles, discouragements, and impossibilities: It is this, that in all things it distinguishes the strong soul from the weak.

—THOMAS CARLYLE (1795–1881),
SCOTTISH WRITER, PHILOSOPHER

My greatest point is my persistence. I never give up in a match. However down I am, I fight until the last ball. My list of matches shows that I have turned a great many so-called irretrievable defeats into victories.

—BJORN BORG (B. 1956), SWEDISH TENNIS PLAYER;
1976–1980 WIMBLEDON MEN'S SINGLES CHAMPION

One of the biggest challenges I have as a teacher is to show my students the power of perseverance. Students today seem to think that the easy way is the best way. I try to set pretty high standards. My curriculum is not easy. It demands that the student come prepared and be able to think through the subjects we study. When a student takes the time to prepare well, when they're persistent in their effort, they find satisfaction and a strengthened belief in their ability to take on more difficult assignments.

—PETER HARRINGTON, NINTH-GRADE GEOGRAPHY
TEACHER, HOUSTON, TEXAS

Nothing in the world can take the place of persistence. Talent will not; nothing is more common than unsuccessful men with talent. Genius will not; unrewarded genius is almost a proverb. Education will not; the world is full of educated derelicts. Persistence and determination alone are omnipotent.

—CALVIN COOLIDGE (1872–1933),
THIRTIETH PRESIDENT OF THE UNITED STATES

One of my students had a hard time with math. As hard as he tried, he simply didn't seem to understand the concepts. It was frustrating to him and to me. I could see he was putting in the effort, which made it all the more disheartening. With the help of a tutor, his parents, and myself, he picked up the principles by seeing the practical applications of math in everyday life. By the end of the first semester he was making Bs. His dedication was itself an inspiration!

—JOANNE SIMPSON, SIXTH-GRADE TEACHER,
BIRMINGHAM, ALABAMA

Kids know the minute you're not being straight with them. They have a sixth sense.

—JAMES JACKSON, SIXTH-GRADE TEACHER,
PORTLAND, OREGON

On the high school level, because of the age and maturity of the students, teachers must be real—students can easily see through the façade of indifference. Very little to no learning takes place when students know a teacher doesn't really care about them as much as they care about their paycheck.

—YVONNE DEAN-GRIFFIN, HIGH SCHOOL FAMILY AND CONSUMER
SCIENCES EDUCATOR, HARTFORD, CONNECTICUT; RECIPIENT
OF THE MILKEN NATIONAL EDUCATOR AWARD

My students see so much deception in the world and their experience that the last place they want to see it is in the classroom. No one's perfect, but to stand in front of twenty-five or thirty students is a great responsibility. Too many kids have lost a sense of right and wrong. If they see a teacher act without regard to rules and regulations, it reinforces this sense. My hope is that by example, in the classroom, they'll see there is a difference and act accordingly.

—GENE PETERSON, MIDDLE SCHOOL COUNSELOR,
SEATTLE, WASHINGTON

CHAPTER 2

Passing the Torch

A teacher affects eternity; they can never tell where their influence stops.

—HENRY ADAMS (1838–1907), PROFESSOR OF MEDIEVAL AND AMERICAN HISTORY AT HARVARD UNIVERSITY AND AUTHOR OF THE AMERICAN CLASSIC *THE EDUCATION OF HENRY ADAMS*

Through us, our educators play a crucial role in shaping the thoughts and ideas of generations to come. The effect a teacher has on the student can never be underestimated. Being a student is a fact of life for most of us from the time we are just past toddling to the time we become adults. The lessons we learn from our teachers we pass on to our children.

Outstanding educators know that their love of teaching and learning came from the encouragement and support of those before them. Learning is an eternal connection broken only when those entrusted with its riches fail to pass them on.

If your plan is for one year, plant rice;
If your plan is for ten years, plant trees;
If your plan is for one hundred years, educate children.

—CONFUCIUS (K'UNG-FU-TZU) (551–479 B.C.),
CHINESE TEACHER, WRITER, AND PHILOSOPHER

Thousands of candles can be lighted from a single candle, and the life of the candle will not be shortened. Happiness never decreases by being shared.

—BUDDHA (568–488 B.C.)

Who so neglects learning in his youth loses the past and is dead to the future.

—EURIPIDES (480–406 B.C.), GREEK PLAYWRIGHT AND TEACHER

Wisdom begins in wonder.

—SOCRATES (469–399 B.C.), GREEK
PHILOSOPHER AND TEACHER OF PLATO

The teacher who is indeed wise in the direction in which education starts a man will determine his future life.

—PLATO (427–347 B.C.), STUDENT OF SOCRATES
AND TEACHER OF ARISTOTLE

Teachers who educate children deserve more honor than parents who merely gave birth. For bare life is furnished by the one, the other ensures a good life.

—ARISTOTLE (384–322 B.C.), TEACHER
TO ALEXANDER THE GREAT

So strong is virtue formed in earlier years.

—VIRGIL (70 B.C.–19 A.D.), ROMAN POET
AND AUTHOR OF THE *AENEID*

He who has imagination without learning has wings and no feet.

—JOSEPH JOUBERT (1754–1824),
FRENCH EDUCATOR AND PHILOSOPHER

In a republic what species of knowledge can be equally important and what duty more pressing on its legislature than to patronize a plan for communicating it to those who are to be the future guardians of the liberties of the country.

—GEORGE WASHINGTON (1732–1799)

The consequences of such establishments we see and feel every day. A native of America who cannot read and write . . . is as rare as a comet or earthquake. It has been observed that we are all of us lawyers, lecturers, politicians, and philosophers. And I have on good authorities to say that all candid foreigners who have passed through this country and conversed freely with all sorts of people here will allow that they have never seen so much knowledge and civility among the common people in any part of the world . . .

The civil and religious principles, therefore, conspired to prompt them to use every measure and take every precaution in their power to propagate and perpetuate knowledge. For this purpose they laid very early the foundations of colleges and invested them with ample privileges and emoluments; and it is remarkable that they have left among their posterity so universal an affection and veneration for those seminaries and for liberal education that the meanest of people contribute cheerfully for the support and maintenance of them every year, and that nothing is more generally popular than projections for the honor, reputation, and advantage of those seats of learning.

—JOHN ADAMS, SECOND PRESIDENT OF THE UNITED STATES, IN *A DISSERTATION ON THE CANON AND FEUDAL LAW* (1765)

To the generous mind the heaviest debt is that of gratitude, when it is not in our power to repay it.

—BENJAMIN FRANKLIN (1706–1790)

Imagination is the living power and prime agent of all human perception.

—SAMUEL TAYLOR COLERIDGE (1772–1834), ENGLISH POET, AUTHOR, AND PHILOSOPHER

This is the true joy in life—that being used for a purpose recognized by yourself as a mighty one. That being a force of nature, instead of a feverish, selfish little clod of ailments and grievances complaining that the world will not devote itself to making you happy. I am of the opinion that my life belongs to the whole community, and as long as I live it is my privilege to do for it whatever I can. I want to be thoroughly used up when I die. For the harder I work the more I live. I rejoice in life for its own sake. Life is no brief candle to me. It's a sort of splendid torch which I've got to hold up for the moment and I want to make it burn as brightly as possible before handing it on to future generations.

—GEORGE BERNARD SHAW (1856–1950),
BRITISH DRAMATIST, PAMPHLETEER, AND
MUSIC, THEATER, AND SOCIAL CRITIC

The man who can make hard things easy is the educator.

—RALPH WALDO EMERSON (1803–1882)

A child is going to carry on what you have started. A child is going to sit where you are sitting and when you are gone, attend to those things you think are important. You may adopt all the policies you please, but how they are carried out depends on that child. Children will assume control over your cities, states, and nations. Children are going to move in and take over your churches, schools, universities, and corporations—the fate of humanity is in their hands.

—ABRAHAM LINCOLN (1809–1865), SIXTEENTH
PRESIDENT OF THE UNITED STATES

Mr. Douglass has very properly chosen to write his own narrative, in his own style, rather than to employ someone else. It is, therefore, entirely his own production; and considering how long and dark the career he had to run as a slave—how few have been his opportunities to improve his mind since he broke his fetters—it is, in my judgment, highly credible to his head and heart.

—WILLIAM LLOYD GARRISON, IN THE PREFACE
TO FREDERICK DOUGLASS'S *AUTOBIOGRAPHIES* (1845)

The frequent hearing of my mistress reading the Bible aloud, for she often read aloud when her husband was absent, awakened by curiosity in respect to this mystery of reading, and aroused in me the desire to learn. Up to this time, I had known nothing whatever of this wonderful art, and my ignorance of what it could do for me . . . emboldened me to ask her to teach me to read . . .

She [Sophia Auld, wife of slave owner Hugh Auld] was, as I have said, naturally a kind and tender-hearted woman, in the humanity of her heart . . . she set out to treat me as she supposed one human ought to treat another.

Of course he [the master] forbade her to give me any further instruction . . . "As to himself, [Auld said,] learning will do him no good, but a great deal of harm, making him disconsolate and unhappy. If you teach him to read, he'll want to know how to write, and this accomplished, he'll be running away with himself . . . " His discourse was the first decidedly anti-slavery lecture to which it had been my lot to listen.

—FREDERICK DOUGLASS, *THE LIFE AND TIMES
OF FREDERICK DOUGLASS* (1881)

I heard so much about Douglass when I was a boy that one of the reasons why I wanted to go to school and learn to read was that I might read for myself what he had written and said.

—BOOKER T. WASHINGTON, FORMER SLAVE AND FOUNDER OF THE TUSKEGEE INSTITUTE, IN *MY LARGER EDUCATION* (1911)

There is only one subject matter for education, and that is life in all of its manifestations.

—ALFRED NORTH WHITEHEAD (1861–1947), PROFESSOR OF PHILOSOPHY AT CAMBRIDGE IN LONDON AND, LATER, AT HARVARD

There will come a time when you believe everything is finished. That will be the beginning.

—LOUIS L'AMOUR (1908–1988), AMERICAN AUTHOR OF WESTERN NOVELS

She left her signature on us, the literature of the teacher who writes on minds. I have had many teachers who told me soon-forgotten facts but only three who created in me a new thing, a new attitude, a new hunger. I suppose that to a large extent I am the unsigned manuscript of that high school teacher. What deathless power lies in the hands of such a person.

—JOHN STEINBECK (1902–1968)

We only learn and act upon what we already know. We create our own reality and walk into the picture we hold of the future.

—VIC LINDAL, VOLLEYBALL COACH FOR SEVERAL
CANADIAN NATIONAL TEAMS AND FOUNDER OF
COMPETITIVE VOLLEYBALL IN CANADA

Karl Marx was sapient enough to deny the impeachment that he was a Marxist. So too Plato was, in my view, a very unreliable Platonist. He was too much of a philosopher to think that anything he had said was the last word. It was left to his disciples to identify his footmarks with his destination.

—GILBERT RYLE, *DILEMMAS* (1972)

As an excellent teacher, she had encouraged comparable qualities in her students and so has helped to set in motion influences that have already had far reaching effects and which will continue for a long time to come.

—JOHN FISHER, FORMER PRESIDENT OF TEACHERS COLLEGE
AT COLUMBIA UNIVERSITY, AT A TESTIMONIAL DINNER FOR
PROFESSOR OF EDUCATION ALICE MIEL (1971)

The best young scholars and teachers are the ones most likely to acknowledge the influence of senior colleagues and teachers in their work. The most satisfied seniors are those who see their own influence in the work of the younger generation.

—JULIUS GETMAN, *IN THE COMPANY OF SCHOLARS* (1992)

To learn means to accept the postulate that life did not begin at my birth. Others have been here before me, and I walk in footsteps. The books I have read were composed by fathers and sons, mothers and daughters, teachers and disciples. I am the sum total of their experiences, their quests. And so are you.

—ELIE WIESEL (B. 1928), WRITER, LECTURER,
AND NAZI CONCENTRATION CAMP SURVIVOR

I'm a counselor who started my career teaching physical education. I came to the teaching profession with determination and a passion to make a difference in the lives of my students.

After several years teaching physical education, I found myself counseling students nearly as often as I did teaching them how to hit a ball, climb a rope, or shoot a basketball. I knew something was missing. I went to the principal and suggested that what our school really needed was a full-time counselor. So, instead of just thinking about it, I went back to school, received a degree in counseling, and have spent the last seventeen years in that position.

The most heartening part of being a counselor is to be able to be a part of the students' life. Over the years I've seen some pretty tough things, but I've also seen how students can overcome difficult times when teachers take an interest in both the academic and personal lives of their students. Letters I receive from graduates make me happy I've chosen this profession.

—BARBARA JONES, MIDDLE SCHOOL COUNSELOR,
MERRIAM, KANSAS

In a completely rational society, the best of us would inspire to be teachers and the rest of us would have to settle for something less, because passing civilization along from one generation to the next ought to be the highest honor and highest responsibility anyone could have.

—LEE IACOCCA, RETIRED CHAIRMAN
OF THE CHRYSLER CORPORATION

The future of education and the goals of schooling must focus on the importance of encouraging learners to have a lifelong commitment to learning, to be responsible for their own learning, to have effective interpersonal and communication skills, to be aware of technology as a tool for learning, and to be effective problem solvers with skills transferable to varied contexts.

—PHILIP C. ABRAMI, PROFESSOR OF PSYCHOLOGY,
UNIVERSITY OF MANITOBA, WINNIPEG, MANITOBA, CANADA

One of the ways I feel that I passed the torch of learning to my students was by being a student myself. My enthusiasm for learning had a positive effect on most of my students. They realized that they too would one day pass on their knowledge to future generations. Without a love of learning, there's not much to pass on.

—ELEANOR SIFT, RETIRED ELEMENTARY
EDUCATOR, VAN NUYS, CALIFORNIA

I cannot tell the truth about anything unless I confess being a student, growing and learning something new every day. The more I learn, the clearer my view of the world becomes.

—SONIA SANCHEZ, AMERICAN POET, EDUCATOR (1934)

The business of teaching is carried forward . . . because some individuals of extraordinary vitality and strength of personality engage in it, and the fire that helps to guide them kindles the spirits of the young people whose lives they touch.

—WOODROW WILSON (1856–1924),
TWENTY-EIGHTH PRESIDENT OF THE UNITED STATES

The neglect of teaching in the university . . . signals a weakening of our will to live. For if we do not nurture our young and identify with them, we forfeit any hope in the regeneration and continuation of our species; we are walled up defensively in the confines of our egos and our momentary gratifications. But this means we are not fully alive ourselves.

—BRUCE WILSHIRE, *THE MORAL COLLAPSE
OF THE UNIVERSITY: PROFESSIONALISM,
PURITY, AND ALIENATION* (1990)

The most important lesson children learn by becoming literate is that they can learn in the way that school endorses learning. Then they join the school society of young learners who use their literacy as currency, as the medium of communication, as tools of thought and deep symbolic play. The bond between teacher and the taught is strengthened; exploration, discovery, ambition, and achievement expand and flourish.

—MARGARET MEEK, PROFESSOR OF ENGLISH, UNIVERSITY OF LONDON INSTITUTE OF EDUCATION, IN *ACHIEVING LITERACY* (1983)

One of the things that I try to do in the classroom is to stimulate the student's imagination. By encouraging them to be better than they thought they could be, and then succeeding at it, they open their minds to all kinds of possibilities.

—BERT TALKINGTON, NINTH-GRADE SCIENCE TEACHER, WHEELING, WEST VIRGINIA

CHAPTER 3

My Favorite Teacher

The object of teaching a child is to enable him to get along without his teacher.

—ELBERT HUBBARD (1856–1915), AMERICAN AUTHOR, SCHOOLTEACHER, LECTURER, JOURNALIST, AND EDITOR OF *THE FRA AND PHILISTINE MAGAZINE*

Many of us know teachers who have had a positive influence on us, changed the course of our lives, demanded that we live up to our potential. Often those teachers never hear from us again, although their influence has been tremendous—on us, our families, and our communities. They were kind, staying late to tutor us, giving an extra word of encouragement when we were down, going out of their way to make sure we learned despite our own determination not to participate in our educations.

But just as often our best teachers were tough. What we thought was meanness or misunderstanding turned out to be a determination to impart lessons not easily learned or to make us perform to our ability. Dan L., a college student from Tupelo, Mississippi, sums up this feeling most aptly when he says, "My toughest teacher expected a lot from me. I think that is why I think fondly of him."

When I was in fifth grade, my teacher, Mrs. Horton, refused to give up on me. I was from a broken home, my parents were recently divorced, and I felt completely lost. My desire to learn and take part in classroom activities was almost nonexistent. Mrs. Horton, realizing my situation, seemed to pay special attention to me. I don't know if she paid more attention to me than the other students. All I know is that her sincere concern and willingness to listen to me helped me through a difficult time. She gave me the desire to "re-enter" life and helped me see that I had a gift and a love for math and science—a gift that I carry with me to this day.

—KEN GRAHAM, CARDIOLOGIST, HARTFORD, CONNECTICUT

One of my most memorable teachers was Dr. Rayburn Moore, who was an English professor at Hendrix College, where I received my undergraduate degree. He inspired me to love learning and literature, and has continued to do research and publish wonderful scholarly books. He continues today to set a sterling example of how scholarship and teaching go hand in hand.

—DR. GLORIA HENDERSON, PROFESSOR OF HUMANITIES,
GORDON COLLEGE, BARNESVILLE, GEORGIA

One teacher really influenced me a lot. She was my high school teacher. Eventually I had the privilege of teaching with her. She was kind, laughed with us, and had a wonderful sense of humor. She made her classes interesting by making us more than an audience of students. We were not just spectators but participants in her class. She brought the subjects to life. Learning with her was like traveling a road by foot. Instead of speeding by in a car, we walked, explored, and took time to understand not only what we learned but why we should learn it. I became a teacher because of her!

—JENNIE HARRISON, SIXTH-GRADE TEACHER,
JACKSONVILLE, FLORIDA

My most memorable teacher was Mr. Ward McAdam, high school music instructor. Ward took a shy, insecure, and self-demeaning young man and helped shape him into someone who could begin to feel pride in both word and deed. He was a compassionate person, filled with a love of his music. Through his demanding expectations and patient tutelage, Ward McAdam was able to coax the best out of the musical illiterates who attended his classes. Of all the teachers I remember, Ward McAdam was the only person who encouraged risk taking, and stood by to help pick me up when the experiment in autonomy went awry. Even now, as I remember him, there's a smile on his face and a tear in my eye. What a wonderful contribution he made to my life and others!

—PROFESSOR MICHAEL WODLINGER, DIRECTOR OF
RESEARCH SERVICES AND GRADUATE STUDIES,
NIPISSING UNIVERSITY, NORTH BAY, CANADA

Dr. Antonio Gennaro comes to my mind when I think of a teacher who changed my life. Dr. Gennaro was my graduate professor and mentor for two years at Eastern New Mexico University. As one of the original seven graduate students for the newly formed Biological Graduate School at Eastern in 1970, he served as my first teaching and mentoring model. Dr. Gennaro was the first professor to believe I could successfully complete a graduate program of studies. He was kind, understanding, helpful, creative, and, most important of all, he believed in me.

—LORENZO GONZALEZ, HIGH SCHOOL TEACHER,
CUBA, NEW MEXICO

In the fall of 1944, I left the cocoon of a small private coed grade school and entered the rough, tough halls of an all-boys Jesuit high school. I was basically shy and kept to myself.

After the initial shock of the first year, I was befriended by a huge (six-foot-four) Jesuit named Father Phil. One of Father Phil's pastimes was taking long walks. On occasion, I would go with him. It was during one of our walks that I learned that he'd been born with a severe speech impediment, stuttering, which he'd overcome to follow his vocation into the Jesuits. It was not easy, but he'd persevered and had become the head of our debate team at school. Mindful of my shyness, he encouraged me to try what he had done.

To this day, I'm not sure why I did. But the results of that decision were remarkable. I began to gain a greater self-confidence. My grades improved and school life started being fun. Later I became a lead in the school play and was elected president of the student council. Father Phil's encouragement to overcome my shyness has paid dividends throughout my life.

—THOMAS MCGEE (B. 1931), FORMER VICE PRESIDENT/
TREASURER, OLD AMERICAN INSURANCE COMPANY

I well remember the best teacher I ever had. He walked three and three-quarter miles every school day from his forty-acre farm to the schoolhouse. He got forty dollars a month during the winter. On Saturdays, he worked in a cooper shop; and in the summer, he looked after his farm. That man, by the very nature of his life, could not teach what is useless.

—HENRY FORD, "THE ONLY REAL SECURITY,"
IN *SATURDAY EVENING POST* (1936)

I'll never forget my art teacher, Mrs. Bee. I met her thirty-four years ago when entering fourth grade. Most kids love to go to art class, and I was no exception. Her projects were creative and practical at the same time. Though I didn't become a professional artist, I received from her a few of life's important lessons, lessons that went far beyond the colorful walls of her classroom. Mrs. Bee believed in me. She challenged me to try new things and explore my creative abilities. She complimented me but also gave constructive criticism when I needed it. She held high expectations for me, and because she believed in me, I always tried to do more than was expected. She also taught me to finish what I started. The life lessons Mrs. Bee taught me may not have made me a famous artist, but they helped me in so many other ways.

—JANE LEE, GEOLOGIST, SAN ANTONIO, TEXAS

My tenth-grade English teacher was remarkable. I don't think I ever learned so much. It wasn't that I learned facts. What I learned were principles of life. Mr. Haskin would give us an assignment to read a play by Shakespeare or a famous novel. Each time we studied the text, he'd come dressed as one of the characters of the book or play. One time he came as Falstaff, the big character in *Henry IV*. Another time he dressed up like Captain Ahab from *Moby Dick*. He wore a big tall hat and carried a harpoonlike pole. He would quote some lines and then ask us to discuss what the character meant and how they fit into the story. His teaching brought the books and plays to life. Even today, whenever I hear the word *Hamlet*, the image of Shakespeare's character comes to mind. I remember Mr. Haskins with a funny-looking outfit and a skull in his hand. He recited the "to be or not to be" passage, and we talked forever about its meaning.

—JOHN SCHLAGLE, SOFTWARE DEVELOPER,
SAN DIEGO, CALIFORNIA

One of my most memorable teachers was my tenth-grade American history teacher. She set the stage for learning history by not only teaching us about the past, but taking us to museums and other historical places. Once, when teaching the Civil War, she took us to two of the battle sites that had been fought in our area. We studied the land formations and the battle strategies employed by both sides. Her teaching made the war more real. I've remained a student of the Civil War ever since.

—RICHARD BROCK, INVESTMENT BANKER,
DALLAS, TEXAS

Miss Dillion was my concert choir and madrigal director in high school. She was demanding and had high expectations. At times it was frustrating because we thought her expectations were too high. But she pushed us because she knew we had the ability to reach higher than we thought we could. Miss Dillion gave us the confidence to reach for the stars. We were like butterflies in a cocoon. The excellence that Miss Dillion demanded from us gave us both confidence and a love of music that is with me to this day.

—NANCY ALBERG, RETIRED ELEMENTARY TEACHER,
LITTLETON, COLORADO

It was a sense of discovery through hands-on experience. My ecology professor, Dr. Dick Meyers of the University of Missouri–Kansas City biology department, taught natural history by poking, prodding, and stomping around in the woods. Tasting berries, sexing live geese by feel, wandering across the Ozark cedar glades in the middle of the night, listening to prairie chickens booming in the predawn, and squirming through cave passages to place bands on screaming bats. That was a delight for a city boy.

—STEVE BAUER, PH.D., FOUNDER AND OWNER OF POCKETWATER,
INC., AN ENVIRONMENTAL CONSULTING FIRM, BOISE, IDAHO

My high school teacher was kind and laughed a lot. For those of us who were into trouble the most, she made us feel valued and never put us down. Her classes were interesting and real. We were not spectators. The lesson belonged to us. Teaching was the furthest thing from my mind. Nursing was a real career choice for me back then. However, I chose teaching because I faint at the sight of blood. I knew that when I taught I could make the classroom a vital place for students to be. It was their classroom and their learning, not my domain and my way. I never view students as "passing through."

—MARION ZAMPA, FIRST-GRADE TEACHER,
OVERLAND PARK, KANSAS

When my daughter was three years old, we enrolled her in a Montessori school. Mrs. White was her teacher, and shortly before Thanksgiving she asked me about my daughter's attention span. She was never disruptive but rarely stayed on track. She simply couldn't follow directions. Sequencing was difficult. Listening to a story was also difficult. Mrs. White hinted that I should have her checked by a specialist. At first I did nothing. This was my firstborn. Deep down I probably knew something was awry. But I did nothing. Time went on and Mrs. White asked me again if I had done anything. Frankly, I was in denial. Somehow I felt that if I gave my daughter more time, she would improve. Shortly after, I checked a local children's hospital for suggestions. It was the best thing I ever did! Tests revealed that she did have learning difficulties. Through a school program and with help from other specialists, my daughter is performing well with modifications. Today she's a confident young girl with a healthy self-esteem.

—DEE MORTON, MOTHER OF TWO,
SEATTLE, WASHINGTON

Every once in a while you stumble upon a good thing. In tenth grade, at a private coeducational school, minicourses were offered after spring break. It was a great idea, and we all scrutinized over what classes we wanted to take. It was a time when spring fever was taking over and a breakup of routine was welcome . . . We received grades, but the classes were elective. Everything was educational, but some courses, like transcendental meditation, were perhaps stretching it a bit.

But it was the two-week TM class, and my instructor, that changed my thinking and helped me become more focused later in school. I learned how to calm myself . . . I learned how to go to sleep at night, even when I was still worked up over something that happened that day. I learned how to think, "I have no pain." I learned the brain is powerful and that I can learn to control it.

TM was taught by my French teacher. She was a wonderful, calm, soft-spoken older lady. Later, I found she liked to do it because it calmed the class and we got much more accomplished when we were relaxed. We, on the other hand, thought we were getting away with something.

You never know what may influence someone's life. It's why as a parent I am willing to expose my children to many different experiences. I applaud teachers who present information creatively, and am grateful to have had them in my past.

—JANIS JENSEN, MOTHER OF FOUR, ATLANTA, GEORGIA

She had a presence that radiated calm integrity. She happened to teach algebra and calculus, but whatever subject she taught would have left a lasting impression, because she truly taught her students.

Her intelligence was apparent immediately. It was finely honed without being sharp; kindness was integral to her presentation. She didn't lecture; she shared a logical progression of ideas. She was patient; she could explain a complex problem from many points of view. She challenged her students to think carefully and deeply; to explore; to consider; to create a logical path to a discovery; and to articulate and document both the process and the result.

She taught in a small-town high school. Her students respected her to the point of awe—whether they enjoyed mathematics or not. She was not large or commanding in stature, but rather ordinary, and as soft looking as her voice. She was not married; it was obvious, even to us at only fourteen, that she treated each student with the respect and high expectations she could have had for her own children. Her dignity and grace, in voice and manner, would almost be considered old-fashioned now, but she was certainly not old in either mind or spirit.

She taught with quiet enthusiasm and extraordinary insight into personal learning styles; she could remember a specific student's difficulties from a class two years previous and mention it with fond and wry humor. After retirement she has continued to be involved in mathematics education, mentoring teachers and volunteering with state teaching organizations. Her students remember her thirty-five years later with affection and gratitude. One student, whose chosen career was not mathematics, started a scholarship in her name, citing this teacher as a continuing influence. Such is the legacy of learning!

—LYNNE HODGMAN, MIXED-MEDIA ARTIST AND TEACHER,
LACONIA, NEW HAMPSHIRE

The job description of a teacher is to help children gain knowledge of subject areas that they do not know, and to do it on the child's level in a manner that they would learn best. Not every child is on the same level, so that means taking large bodies of information and trying to tailor them to each student. So we can see that what the child brings or doesn't bring to school with him or her can have a large bearing on how well he or she learns.

What "extras" teachers have coming at them also make teaching a true juggling act. Teachers need to be equipped with large doses of organization, patience, humor, and love for children.

For the amount of hours worked compared to the amount of pay they receive, teachers deserve a special place in heaven. We should be forever grateful to the many people who have dedicated their years of teaching to our children. We are all the richer for it.

—JANE LEACH, MOTHER OF THREE,
OVERLAND PARK, KANSAS

CHAPTER 4

Turn on the Light

Beware lest you lose the substance by grasping at the shadow.

—AESOP (620?–560? B.C.),
GREEK FORMER THRACIAN SLAVE
AND AUTHOR OF FABLES

Without light, the path before us is hard to walk. All the facts and figures in the world don't help us illuminate the path we have to take in life. Yet, when a teacher trips the light switch of our minds, we begin to experience and better see the road of learning. Teachers who "turn on the light" help students see the connection between theory and practice, between ideas and applications. They are the ones who help us activate the beacons of light against darkness.

One must learn by doing the thing, for though you think you know it, you have no certainty until you try.

—ARISTOTLE (384–322 B.C.)

Grasp the subject, the words will follow.

—CATO THE ELDER (95–46 B.C.), ROMAN
STATESMAN AND PHILOSOPHER

The greatest loss of time is delay and expectation, which depends upon the future. We let go the present, which we have in our power, and look forward to that which depends upon chance, and so relinquish a certainty for an uncertainty.

—SENECA THE YOUNGER (5 B.C.–67 A.D.), ROMAN TEACHER
WHOSE BOOKS THE *TENNE TRAGEDIES* WOULD INFLUENCE
THE ELIZABETHAN WRITERS OF THE 16TH CENTURY

Once children learn how to learn, nothing is going to narrow their minds.

—HORACE MANN (1796–1859), AMERICAN EDUCATOR WHO
ESTABLISHED THE MASSACHUSETTS STATE BOARD OF EDUCATION

Education consists of mainly what we have unlearned.

—MARK TWAIN, *MARK TWAIN'S NOTEBOOK*,
EDITED BY ALBERT BIGELOW PAINE (1924)

The arbitrary training given to memory was stupefying; the strain that the memory endured was a form of torture; and the feats that the boys performed, without complaint, were pitiable. No other faculty than the memory seemed to be recognized. Least of all was any use made of reason, either analytic, synthetic, or dogmatic. The German government did not encourage reasoning.

—HENRY ADAMS, *THE EDUCATION OF HENRY ADAMS* (1905)

The great waste comes from [the child's] inability to utilize the experiences he gets outside of school in any complete and free way within the school itself while, on the other hand, he is unable to apply in daily life what he is learning at school. That is the isolation of the school—its isolation from life.

JOHN DEWEY, *THE CHILD AND THE CURRICULUM AND THE SCHOOL AND SOCIETY* (1900)

These are not books, lumps of paper, but "minds" alive on the shelves. From each of them goes its own voice.

—GILBERT HIGHET, AUTHOR OF THE SEMINAL WORK ON TEACHING METHOD, *THE ART OF TEACHING* (1950)

In the case of good books, the point is not to see how many of them you can get through, but how many get through to you.

—MORTIMER ADLER (B. 1902), PHILOSOPHER, EDUCATOR, AND THE ORIGINATOR AND EDITOR OF THE GREAT BOOKS PROGRAM AT THE UNIVERSITY OF CHICAGO

Teaching is most effective not when it succeeds in transmitting the greatest quantity of information in the shortest time (and at lowest cost) but rather when most of the information conveyed by the teacher is actually received.

—PIERRE BOURDIEU AND JEAN-CLAUDE PASSERON, *RAPPORT PÉDAGOGIQUE ET COMMUNICATION* (1965)

Reaching the next level of understanding brings with it real excitement—it's a blast to expand your mind. Many students, of course, don't know that. So I convey that energy and elation by showing my own excitement when they reveal breakthroughs in their own learning, and it's contagious.

I often teach required classes that students are pre-disposed to resent. I change students' prejudices about the class by showing that it can be exciting from the first day—not the boring formulaic exercise they might expect. For instance, I teach a lot of introductory writing classes, and students expect me to lecture about grammar. But the first day, I say, "This class is about how to take your ideas and articulate them in powerful ways so that you earn the respect of everyone with whom you communicate. This class isn't about commas and semicolons; it's about power. Language is power, the tool you use to crack into the brains of those you want to hear you, understand you, respect you."

—WILLIAM B. LALICKER, ENGLISH PROFESSOR, WEST CHESTER UNIVERSITY, WEST CHESTER, PENNSYLVANIA

Consider the similarities between performing artists and teachers; both have an audience; both have a place to perform; each has a wide variety of ways to perform; each has an instrument to be used . . . the intent of an artist performer is to entertain, but the performance may also instruct. The intent of the teacher is to instruct, but his or her performance may also entertain.

—LEON M. LESSINGER AND DON GILLIS,
TEACHING AS A PERFORMING ART (1976)

There are only two lasting bequests we could hope to give our children. One is these is roots; the other is wings.

—HODDING CARTER III, ASSISTANT SECRETARY OF PUBLIC
AFFAIRS UNDER PRESIDENT JIMMY CARTER, 1976–1980

We can, with John Dewey, conceive of "mind as a verb rather than a noun," and can thereby be open to the possibility of attentiveness, engagement, and action.

—WILLIAM AYERS, "DOING PHILOSOPHY: MAXINE GREEN AND THE
PEDAGOGY OF POSSIBILITY," IN *TEACHERS AS MENTORS* (1994)

Students should understand before the lesson begins what is to be mastered by the end. No one starts out on a journey without an idea where they'll end up. In my classroom, I try to give the students a clear picture where we expect to end up.

—BARBARA JORGENSON, FOURTH-GRADE TEACHER,
PHOENIX, ARIZONA

See the way and you see the end. Not understanding all the logistical and marketing components that make up a successful enterprise is a recipe for disaster.

—MARK FEIDEN, INTERNET SPECIALIST, DESCRIBING THE DEFINING PRINCIPLE OF ESTABLISHING AN E-COMMERCE BUSINESS

Good comprehension is the result of a solid beginning. Before beginning the lesson, lead into the text or video with an introduction. Let the students know what topics will be covered.

—JANICE McCLAREN, THIRD-GRADE TEACHER, CINCINNATI, OHIO

In making art, I ask the children to think about themselves and to paint or draw from their personal experience. They learn to apply their art knowledge to the creation of their image and to think about the process of art as a conversation between the artist, materials, and idea.

—BRUCE HUCKO, CHILDREN'S "ART COACH" AND AUTHOR

A student needs an instantaneous mental picture of the whole point before settling down for analysis or participation. Comprehension comes only with understanding. If there is no foundation, there can be no understanding and, ultimately, no comprehension . . .

I have found that students will simply turn off if a question remains unanswered. Being alert to attitudes on the part of the teacher goes a long way to having a satisfactory lesson or a complete waste of time. An unanswered question is a mental block that is hard to overcome.

—CHARLES WOOTTEN, SEVENTH-GRADE TEACHER, PETERSBURG, VIRGINIA

I have encountered very few students in my thirty-plus years of teaching who flunked out because they didn't have the mental ability for the academic enterprise. If you attend class consistently, read your assignments carefully, take notes, and run a little scared as you study for the exams— if you take your class seriously and focus on your semester-long task—you really can't miss. You will do just fine.

—THAYLE ANDERSON, PROFESSOR OF ENGLISH AND GRADUATE STUDIES, MURRAY STATE UNIVERSITY, MURRAY, KENTUCKY

I walk around the room to read the responses as my students are predicting what they think the answer is to our science question and why. These responses let me know the prior knowledge or misconceptions of each student before I begin. At the end of a class we do a small group and large group summary of ideas. I constantly check for understanding while students are completing an activity in their group by asking leading questions. I always give students the opportunity to question each other and me.

—ANNE M. HOLBROOK, K–6 AND COLLEGE GRADUATE SCIENCE TEACHER, PRINCETON CITY SCHOOLS; ALBERT EINSTEIN DISTINGUISHED EDUCATOR FELLOW

Treat me like I'm my age.

—LUCY HILL, NINTH GRADE, YONKERS, NEW YORK

It is not the answer that enlightens, but the question.

—EUGENE IONESCO (1909–1994), FRENCH
PLAYWRIGHT BORN IN ROMANIA

The wise man doesn't give the right answers, he poses the right questions.

—CLAUDE GUSTAVE LÉVI-STRAUSS (B. 1908),
FRENCH ANTHROPOLOGIST

I try to allow students extra time to think and reflect. It's especially important in a time so fast-paced and filled with activities. By giving them extra time, or pausing between topics, they seem to integrate what I'm teaching better. They become less concerned about getting to the next subject.

—PAM MARTIN, SEVENTH-GRADE TEACHER,
MINNEAPOLIS, MINNESOTA

Reading is to the mind what exercise is to the body.

—RICHARD STEELE (1672–1729),
ENGLISH PLAYWRIGHT

An education isn't how much you have committed to memory, or even how much you know. It's being able to differentiate between what you do know and what you don't.

—ANATOLE FRANCE, FRENCH SATIRIST AND
1921 NOBEL LAUREATE

All life is only a set of pictures in the brain.

—H. P. LOVECRAFT (1890–1937), AMERICAN
JOURNALIST, NOVELIST, AND GHOSTWRITER

The image is the great instrument of instruction. What a child gets out of any subject presented to him is simply the images that he himself forms with regard to it. If nine-tenths of the energy spent on instruction were spent in seeing to it that the child was forming proper images, the work of instruction would be indefinitely facilitated.

—JOHN DEWEY, *MODERN EDUCATION* (1930)

The most useful and common interaction between exception and memory takes place in the recognition of things seen.

—RUDOLF ARNHEIM, PROFESSOR EMERITUS OF THE
PSYCHOLOGY OF ART, HARVARD UNIVERSITY

I have found that by deviating from a well-accepted lesson design students become more responsible for their own education. The typical lesson calls for an introduction, the lesson, and then a summary. By leaving off the summary, students are forced to start summarizing the material themselves, breaking away from a dependency on the teacher. I think this is how my brother, Willis, and I both teach. Students comment "never again will I memorize the material." They basically begin to think about what they are learning. Once students begin to think for themselves, they are beginning to become individuals who accept responsibility for their actions. Self-confidence is one of the natural outcomes when individuals accept responsibility.

—LAVOIR BANKS, RETIRED PROFESSOR OF CHEMISTRY,
BRIGHAM YOUNG UNIVERSITY, OGDEN, UTAH

CHAPTER 5

It's a Big World

From a neurological standpoint, it's harder to be a kid than an adult. Kids are asked to be generalists in school, to do everything fairly well. We adults don't ask that of ourselves.

—MEL LEVINE, "ALL CHILDREN GREAT AND SMALL," IN *TEACHER MAGAZINE* (2001)

It's not the same for everybody.

—MICHAEL D., SEVENTH GRADE, WHEELING, WEST VIRGINIA

We live in a world of endless variety. Never is this complexity more clearly seen than in the classroom. No two students think or learn the exact same way. While one student may grasp the facts of math, the same student may have difficulty with spelling. Another may understand mathematical concepts but have difficulty putting them together. It's important to recognize these differences, as well as our own, when confronting the challenges of the classroom.

In teaching there should be no class distinctions.

—CONFUCIUS (K'UNG-FU-TZU) (551–479 B.C.),
CHINESE TEACHER, WRITER, AND PHILOSOPHER

Numberless are the world's wonders, but none more wonderful than man.

—SOPHOCLES, ANTIGONE (442 B.C.)

He would beat us unmercifully . . . He would ask a boy a question, and if he did not answer him, he would beat him, he would beat him without considering whether he had an opportunity of knowing how to answer it . . . Now sir, if a boy could answer every question, there would be no need of a master to teach him.

—SAMUEL JOHNSON, ENGLISH NOVELIST, POET, PHILOSOPHER,
AND LEXICOGRAPHER, ON THE HEADMASTER OF LITCHFIELD
SCHOOL, MR. HUNTER, JOHNSON'S LATIN TEACHER IN 1725

The strongest principle of growth lies in human choice.

—GEORGE ELIOT (1818–1880),
ENGLISH NOVELIST

The highest result of education is tolerance.

—HELEN KELLER, *OPTIMISM* (1903)

With a book in my hand so redolent of the principles of liberty, with a perception of my own human nature and the facts of my past and present experience, I was equal to a contest with the religious advocates of slavery, whether white or black, for blindness in this matter was not confined to white people . . .

Educate the poor white children and the colored children together; let them grow up to know that color makes no difference as to the rights of man; that both the black man and the white man are at home; that the country is as much of one as of the other, and the both together must make it a valuable country.

—FREDERICK DOUGLASS, *THE LIFE AND TIMES OF FREDERICK DOUGLASS* (1881)

The majority of successful men are persons who have had difficulties to overcome, problems to master; and in overcoming those difficulties and mastering those problems, they have gained strength of mind and a clearness of vision that few persons who have had a life of ease have been able to attain.

—BOOKER T. WASHINGTON, *MY LARGER EDUCATION* (1911)

Power consists in one's capacity to link his will with the purpose of others, to lead by reason and a gift of cooperation.

—WOODROW WILSON, TWENTY-EIGHTH PRESIDENT OF THE UNITED STATES, IN A LETTER TO MARY A. HULBERT (1913)

Teaching can be compared to selling commodities. No one can sell unless someone buys . . . [yet] there are teachers who think they have done a good day's teaching irrespective of what pupils have learned.

—JOHN DEWEY, *HOW WE THINK* (1933)

There are nine and sixty ways of teaching these days, and everyone of them is right!

—CLAUDE M. FUESS, *CREED OF A SCHOOL MASTER* (1939)

All things being equal, the mixed school is the broader, more natural basis for the education of all youth; it inspires greater self-confidence; and suppresses the inferiority complex.

—W. E. B. DU BOIS, "A NEGRO NATION WITHIN THE NATION," IN *THE CRISIS* (1953)

We can no longer teach using one way because we have learned that children don't learn one way. As teachers we need a bag full of tricks to reach and motivate our students. Many different approaches, projects, hands-on learning, visual and auditory methods have to be utilized.

—ALAN GIBBY, HEAD OF INTERMEDIATE AND MIDDLE SCHOOLS, COLUMBIA, SOUTH CAROLINA

There are many who lust for the simple answers of doctrine or decree. They are on the left and right. They are not confined to a single part of society. They are terrorists of the mind.

—A. BARTLETT GIAMATTI, AMERICAN SCHOLAR OF RENAISSANCE
LITERATURE, PRESIDENT OF YALE UNIVERSITY, AND COMMISSIONER
OF MAJOR LEAGUE BASEBALL, IN *THE NEW YORK TIMES* (1975)

So long as materials are taught and assessed in only one way, we will only reach a certain kind of child. But everything can be taught in several ways. The more that we can match youngsters to congenial approaches of teaching, learning, and assessing, the more likely it is that those youngsters will achieve educational success.

—HOWARD GARDNER (B. 1943), PROFESSOR, GRADUATE SCHOOL OF
EDUCATION, HARVARD UNIVERSITY, CAMBRIDGE, MASSACHUSETTS

Faced with diversity and confusion, humans try to group things, and will certainly do that to lists of strategies.

—R. T. WHITE, *EDUCATIONAL RESEARCH, METHODOLOGY,
AND MEASUREMENT* (1988)

So often, as teachers and parents, we look at children's creations and see what they cannot do. We are so shocked by misspellings that we cannot see the writing. With younger children, we are most tolerant, but as the children grow older misspellings worry us. We wonder what people will think if they read something as badly spelled as some of the writing the children produce . . . Yet, the children's spellings so progress . . . As children write, they practice essential reading skills.

—CATHY ROLLER, *VARIABILITY, NOT DISABILITY* (1996)

The work done in the little classroom of the distant county or in the big classroom of a great city is essentially the same—it is the work of changing American children into good American men and women, physically, socially, economically self-sufficient, believing in equality because they have known it, believing in opportunity for others because they have experienced opportunity, and believing in each other because, through childhood studies, they have been directly and intimately associated with each other as part of the people.

—GUY PRATT DAVIS, *WHAT SHALL THE PUBLIC SCHOOLS DO FOR THE FEEBLE MINDED?* (1927)

On leaving the newsroom and entering the classroom, I knew that I'd have to work on being patient. Deadline pressures and the swiftness of gratification—seeing stories in print the following morning—just don't exist in the classroom. The only pressure I have is self-imposed, and because I'm in charge of the order and pace of the semester, I can change it at any time.

I am, however, learning that the oft-spoken rewards that accrue to teachers—the joy of seeing accomplishment, the sheer pleasure of seeing "that light go on"—do come as I exercise patience. I have to realize first that I wasn't nearly as good during my college years as my faulty memory recalls. I have to realize that each generation of students is the product of schools and circumstances that yield good kids, mediocre kids, and bad kids. I have to be patient and accept the differences.

—Gerald B. Jordan, associate professor, Walter J. Lemke
Department of Journalism, University of Arkansas

Problems that fostered the old one-room school practice are still with us today: a wide variation in ability and too many students in each classroom. The basic problems with the old practice can be greatly reduced by appropriate training. The older (student's) attitude toward school can be reversed, and he can make school more attractive to the younger. The older child can be taught what younger children are like, and can acquire techniques that improve the younger child's learning.

—Peggy Lippert, "Learning Through Cross-Age Helping,"
in *Children As Teachers* (1976)

The children entering your class each autumn differ greatly in experiential background and in intellectual, social, and emotional maturation. They grow in different ways and achieve different results. Therefore, each child should choose his own material [for quiet reading time] and read at his own rate rather than gear his reading to the interest and reading rate of the group.

—*Prentice-Hall Teachers Encyclopedia* (1970)

A teacher must be able to identify the skill levels of each student in the room in order to teach an intellectually diverse class.

I tend to test the skills of my students very early on in the year to be able to identify the intellectual levels that I have. I make use of any support resources that my school may have and make sure my students who need extra help are getting it. I take a lesson and incorporate higher-level thinking questions for the students who need to be challenged more.

—Mary Ransone, retired second-grade
teacher, Memphis, Tennessee

Some children do not hear well, others don't see well; some have limitation on their perceptual input, integrative, and output mechanisms. Any one or combinations of these curtail and, if extreme, eliminate, the quantity and quality of participation in the communication process.

—Muska Mosston, *Teaching* (1972)

Both the dreamer and the child who seeks attention through aggression may have reading problems. One is seeking escape from this insolvable problem, and the other is trying to compensate for his feelings of inferiority. The teacher who is able to help these children must have a deep interest in them and a great amount of patience.

—Lewis Knowles, *Encouraging Talk* (1983)

I believe my daughter has excelled because of the positive classroom environment set by her teachers. In art class, for example, her project didn't look like many of the other children's work, but her use of color was subtle and dramatic. The teacher praised my daughter's work in front of her and her peers. I think the praise supports her sense of self-worth. It is a wonderful thing to observe a teacher who makes it a point to mention strengths when other students can overhear. Differences, when seen as strengths instead of weaknesses, can help motivate all students.

—DONNA AMIS, PARENT OF A CHILD WITH LEARNING DIFFERENCES, PRAIRIE VILLAGE, KANSAS

The students I taught were all adults, so they had a different set of demands and challenges at home than elementary or high school students. When they were having problems at home, I told them first that what they're doing was remarkable. Few adults undertake the challenge to work, take care of a family, and continue their education. It's something that at the time you wonder how you're going to get through but later you can look back on with pride.

Then I told them something they usually found shocking—that afterwards, no one will care whether they got a C or an A in my class. Grades really didn't matter. They may have turned in a paper that wasn't their best work or they did poorly on a test, but they're still learning. It's essential to remember at those times why they're in school—to expand their knowledge. That's the only thing that counts.

—CHRISTI CLEMONS HOFFMAN, ENGLISH TEACHER, FORMERLY OF ECOLE ZARADI, GENEVA, SWITZERLAND

Historically, the focus of remediation has been one of separating out and starting over. A reading specialist's job is seen as searching out children who fail and re-instructing—repeating particularly those easily identified bits and pieces of reading, the "skills" . . . and the children, the struggling readers for whom good instruction can make the most difference, become less able.

—MARY DAYTON SAHARI, IN THE FOREWORD
TO *VARIABILITY, NOT DISABILITY* (1996)

Do not call for black power or green power. Call for brain power.

—BARBARA JORDAN, LAWYER, TEXAS STATE REPRESENTATIVE,
1966–1972; U.S. REPRESENTATIVE, 1972–1978

Disadvantaged students—An imprecise category of intellectually and physically normal students whose economic and cultural circumstances are among the lowest in the United States. Depending on the community, the ranking may vary from the lowest one-third to the lowest 10 percent.

—*ENCYCLOPEDIA OF AMERICAN EDUCATION* (1996)

The image is the great instrument of instruction. What a child gets out of any subject presented to him is simply the images that he himself forms with regard to it. If nine-tenths of the energy spent on instruction were spent in seeing to it that the child was forming proper images, the work of instruction would be indefinitely facilitated.

—JOHN DEWEY, *MODERN EDUCATION* (1930)

We had to learn to visualize from a very early age. We didn't have TV and spent much of our leisure time listening to the radio and reading books. I particularly loved listening to radio situation comedies like Jack Benny, mysteries like The Shadow, and westerns like the Lone Ranger. Our family and friends would sit around the radio, visualize the story, and have a great time.

—PAT JOHNSON, GRANDMOTHER, WILMINGTON, DELAWARE

All I really need to know about how to live and what to do and how to be I learned in kindergarten. Remember the Dick-and-Jane books and the first word you learned—the biggest word of all—look.

—ROBERT FULGHUM, AMERICAN AUTHOR, *ALL I REALLY NEEDED TO KNOW I LEARNED IN KINDERGARTEN* (1988)

We know that every child doesn't learn the same way. In my classroom, when we are planning an art project we will plan in images and in words because we all think differently. Some think in pictures and some think in words.

—ELLEN TAYLOR, MIDDLE SCHOOL ART TEACHER, OLATHE, KANSAS

Recently, I asked my students after reading a passage in our social studies book what they thought they heard. I was amazed at how they "saw" things differently. So, we divided into smaller groups to discuss their own imaging of each of the phrases or words. I think it was the first time most of them actually thought about how they think and remember.

—JODY JOHNSON, FIFTH-GRADE TEACHER, PORTLAND, OREGON

In teaching "the basics" to any group, it is important to realize that one person's basics is seldom
another person's and almost never everyone's . . .

If there is one standard for success in a classroom
then, in all probability, a teacher is not required but a
drill sergeant might be.

—LT. COL. MIKE SCHAEFER, U.S. ARMY RESERVES,
COMMAND AND GENERAL STAFF COLLEGE TRAINING BATTALION

Washington Irving Junior High is a school with a diverse
population of students and they are heterogeneously mixed.
The biggest challenge I face is finding a common experience
base from which to work. Some students have never been
out of the city and others have traveled around the world.
Some are ready for formal algebra and some are still struggling with their times tables. I start off with activities that
assess academic strengths and weaknesses while encouraging students to work cooperatively as they solve problems.
As I ascertain common experiences, I build on these to
introduce mathematical concepts, establish a rigorous
vocabulary, and instill the idea that we have a common goal
of learning mathematics.

—JOHN D. PUTNAM, RETIRED SEVENTH- TO NINTH-GRADE MATH
TEACHER; RECIPIENT OF THE MILKEN NATIONAL EDUCATOR AWARD

Each of us learns, comprehends, and retains at a different
pace and in different ways.

—PETER TOMPKINS, PH.D., ROCHESTER, NEW YORK

In the information age, you don't teach philosophy as they did after feudalism. You perform it. If Aristotle were alive today, he'd have a talk show.

—Timothy Leary (1920–1996),
American psychologist and author

Know who your students are and use that knowledge. With 150 students a day rotating through my classroom, it would seem impossible to really get to know them. Using a hands-on approach to lesson planning gives me the time to "work the room" on a regular basis while they are busy with their projects. You can learn a lot just by observing them at work, but taking a few minutes to talk to each student during a week will allow you to build great background.

—Kay Lehmann, eighth-grade social studies teacher,
Walla Walla, Washington; recipient of
the Milken National Educator Award

Understanding and utilizing multiple intelligences in the classroom can open doors to learning and success for many students who might otherwise find it too difficult, boring, or meaningless to do their best in school . . . This sense of validation and the emotional positive connections that multiple intelligence instruction promotes may well be one of its greatest strengths as an instructional strategy.

—Joan Caulfield, Center for the Advancement
of Reform in Education, Rockhurst University,
Kansas City, Missouri, and Dr. Wayne Jennings,
Designs for Learning, St. Paul, Minnesota

The environment in which the brain operates determines to a large extent the functioning ability of that brain.

—Dr. Marian Diamond, professor of anatomy, University of California at Berkeley

For me teaching is not about parts and pieces, but about empowerment. I feel my goal as a teacher is to help kids recognize their capabilities, develop their desire to grow, and then support those efforts as they learn. How this is done is different for each and every person.

—Brian Colter, eighth-grade resource teacher, Long Island, New York

Many highly intelligent people are poor thinkers. Many people of average intelligence are skilled thinkers. The power of a car is separate from the way the car is driven.

—Dr. Edward De Bono, educator, author, Rhodes Scholar; regarded as the world's leading authority in creative thinking

CHAPTER 6

Thoughts for Students and Teachers

"Jule," my father would say, "until you learn to be a good pinochle player you will never be a real man." At that, he may have been right. I never did become a real man. But I doubt if pinochle had anything to do with it.

—GROUCHO MARX, *GROUCHO AND ME* (1959)

We all look for the right words for students. When these fail, the advice and wisdom of those who came before and those around us are a great help. Sometimes just gaining a little perspective on what we are doing will help us loosen the tongue and say the right thing. Still other times, quiet understanding is best.

A memorable word or thoughtful phrase can often cause us to pause and think, to reflect and wonder about the world around us. Such inspiration is relevant to both the students who need the motivation and the teachers who need the inspiration to reach students.

The jade uncut will not form a vessel for use; and if men do not learn, they do not know the way in which they should go. On this account the ancient kings, when establishing states and governing the people, make instruction and schools a primary object; the thoughts from the first to the last should be fixed on learning.

—CONFUCIUS (K'UNG-FU-TZU) (551–479 B.C.)

Do nothing you do not understand.

—PYTHAGORAS (569?–475 B.C.), IONIAN MATHEMATICIAN

There is nothing more dreadful than the habit of doubt. Doubt separates people. It is a poison that disintegrates friendships and breaks up pleasant relations. It is a thorn that irritates and hurts; it is a sword that kills.

—BUDDHA (568–488 B.C.)

Who so neglects learning in his youth loses the past and is dead for the future.

—EURIPIDES (485–406 B.C.), GREEK PLAYWRIGHT

A good education consists of giving to the body and to the soul all the beauty and all the perfection of which they are capable.

—PLATO (427–347 B.C.)

Great knowledge you have gained from books, 'tis true,
But don't forget that life can teach you something too.

—MARCUS PORCIUS CATO, AKA CATO THE ELDER (234–149 B.C.),
ROMAN SOLDIER, SENATOR, AND STATESMAN

Natural ability without education has more often raised a man to glory and virtue than education without natural ability.

—MARCUS TULLIUS CICERO (106–43 B.C.),
ROMAN ORATOR AND STATESMAN

Men do not care how nobly they live, but only how long, although it is within the reach of every man to live nobly, but within no man's power to live long.

—LUCIUS ANNAEUS SENECA, *EPISTULAE AD LUCILIUM* (63–64 A.D.)

If you are distressed by anything external, the pain is not due to the thing itself but to your own estimate of it; and this you have the power to revoke at any moment.

—MARCUS AURELIUS (121–180 A.D.), ROMAN STOIC PHILOSOPHER

Begin—to begin is half the work, let half still remain; again begin this, and thou wilt have finished.

—DECIMUS MAGNUS AUSONIUS (310?–395? A.D.),
LATIN POET AND RHETORITICIAN

Every habit and every faculty is confirmed and strengthened by the corresponding act; the faculty of walking by walking; that of running by running. If you wish to have a faculty for reading, read; if for writing, write.

—EPICTETUS (55?–135 A.D.), GREEK AUTHOR AND STOIC
PHILOSOPHER, IN *THE DISCOURSES OF EPICTETUS*

Each man is the smith of his own fortune

—APPIUS CLAUDIUS CAECUS (312 A.D.–?), ROMAN CENSUS
ADMINISTRATOR AFTER WHOM THE APPIAN WAY WAS NAMED

To have another language is to possess a second soul.

—CHARLEMAGNE (742–814 A.D.), FIRST
EMPEROR OF THE HOLY ROMAN EMPIRE

One must know oneself. If this does not serve to discover truth, it at least serves as a rule of life and there is nothing better.

—BLAISE PASCAL (1623–1662), FRENCH
PHILOSOPHER AND MATHEMATICIAN

Great works are performed not by strength but by perseverance.

—SAMUEL JOHNSON (1709–1784), ENGLISH NOVELIST,
POET, PHILOSOPHER, AND LEXICOGRAPHER

Whatever you can do or dream you can, begin it. Boldness has genius, power, and magic it.

—JOHANN WOLFGANG VON GOETHE (1749–1832),
GERMAN POET, DRAMATIST, NOVELIST, AND SCIENTIST

Associate with men of good quality if you esteem your own reputation; for it is better to be alone than in bad company.

—GEORGE WASHINGTON (1732–1799)

I like the dreams of the future better than the history of the past.

—THOMAS JEFFERSON (1743–1826),
THIRD PRESIDENT OF THE UNITED STATES

What is really important in education is not that the child becomes this and that, but that the mind is matured, that energy is aroused.

—SØREN KIERKEGAARD, DANISH PHILOSOPHER
AND THEOLOGIAN, *EITHER/OR* (1843)

The artist who aims at perfection in everything achieves it in nothing.

—EUGÈNE DELACROIX (1798–1863), FRENCH PAINTER

Without ambition one starts nothing. Without work one finishes nothing. The prize will not be sent to you. You have to win it. The man who knows how will always have a job. The man who also knows why will always be his boss. As to methods there may be a million and then some, but principles are few. The man who grasps principles can successfully select his own methods. The man who tries methods, ignoring principles, is sure to have trouble.

—RALPH WALDO EMERSON (1803–1882)

Education is the instruction of the intellect in the laws of nature, under which I include not merely things and their forces, but men and their ways, the fashioning of the affections and of the will into an earnest and living desire to move in harmony with these laws.

—THOMAS HENRY HUXLEY (1825–1895),
ENGLISH SCIENTIST AND AUTHOR

We should be careful to get out of an experience only the wisdom that is in it—and stop there; lest we be like the cat that sits down on a hot stove-lid. She will never sit down on a hot stove-lid again—and that is well; but also she will never sit down on a cold one anymore.

—MARK TWAIN (1835–1910)

I have learned that success is to be measured not so much by the position that one has reached in life as by the obstacles which he has overcome while trying to succeed.

—BOOKER T. WASHINGTON (1856–1915), FORMER
SLAVE AND FOUNDER OF THE TUSKEGEE INSTITUTE

At the utmost, the active-minded young man should ask of his teacher only mastery of his tools. The young man himself, the subject of education, is a certain form of energy. The object to be gained is economy of his force; the training is partly the cleaning away of obstacles, partly the direct application of effort. Once acquired, the tools and the models may be thrown away.

—HENRY ADAMS, *THE EDUCATION
OF HENRY ADAMS* (1905)

Failure is only the opportunity to begin again more intelligently.

—HENRY FORD (1863–1947)

Failure is instructive. The person who really thinks learns quite as much from his failures as from his successes.

—JOHN DEWEY (1859–1952)

After all, I do only want to advise you to keep growing quietly and seriously throughout your whole development; you cannot disturb it more rudely than by looking outward and expecting from outside, replies to questions that only your innermost feeling in your most hushed hour can perhaps answer.

—RAINER MARIA RILKE (1875–1926),
GERMAN WRITER AND POET

Either you think—or else others have to think for you and take power from you, prevent and discipline your natural tastes, civilize and sterilize you.

—F. SCOTT FITZGERALD,
TENDER IS THE NIGHT (1934)

Don't just grab at the first thing that comes along. Have an idea in your head and be willing to wait for it. Knowing when to refuse something that won't get you anywhere. Struggling along for years, you got to wait for a thing till it is ripe; don't just jump into things just because somebody offers it to you. Look and see if it's going to lead you anywhere.

—WILL ROGERS (1879–1935)

Every man and woman is born into the world to do something unique and something distinctive and if he or she does not do it, it will never be done.

—BENJAMIN E. MAYS (1895–1984),
AMERICAN EDUCATOR, CLERGYMAN

Not everything that can be counted counts, and not everything that counts can be counted.

—ALBERT EINSTEIN (1879–1955)

Money is only a tool. It will take you wherever you wish, but it will not replace you as the driver.

—AYN RAND, RUSSIAN-BORN AMERICAN AUTHOR OF *THE FOUNTAINHEAD* (1943) AND *ATLAS SHRUGGED* (1957)

We could never learn to be brave and patient, if there were only joy in the world.

—HELEN KELLER (1880–1968),
AMERICAN WRITER AND LECTURER

Real education should educate us out of self into something far finer—into selflessness which links us with all humanity.

—MARY ASTOR (1906–1987),
AMERICAN FILM ACTRESS

In Topeka, as a small child, my mother took me with her to the little vine-covered library on the grounds of the Capitol . . . The silence inside the library, the big chairs, and long tables, and the fact that the library was always there and didn't seem to have a mortgage on it, or any sort of insecurity about it—all of that made me love it. And right there, even before I was six, books began to happen to me, so that after a while, there came a time when I believed in books more than people—which, of course, was wrong.

—LANGSTON HUGHES, *The Big Sea* (1940)

How long had I been pure in my life-work and how had I come so confidently to survey and plan it? I now realize that most college seniors are by no means certain of what they want to do or can do with life; but stand rather upon a hesitating threshold awaiting will, chance, or opportunity.

—W. E. B. DU BOIS, *What the Negro Wants* (1944)

A day spent without sight and sound of beauty, the contemplation of mystery, or the search for truth and perfections is a poverty stricken day; and a succession of such days is fatal to human life.

—LEWIS MUMFORD, AMERICAN SOCIAL SCIENTIST, IN *The Condition of Man* (1944)

To be surprised, to wonder, is to begin to understand.

—JOSÉ ORTEGA Y GASSETT,
THE REVOLT OF THE MASSES (1930)

The idea that it is necessary to go to a university in order to become a successful writer or even a man or woman of letters (which is by no means the same thing) is one of the phantasies that surrounds authorship.

—VERA BRITTAIN, *ON BEING AN AUTHOR* (1948)

Both teachers and pupils at sixteenth-century universities had dressed and looked like clergymen even when they were not. Both professors and students at the seventeenth-century universities disguised themselves as gentlemen, even when they were not.

—PRESERVED SMITH, *A HISTORY OF MODERN CULTURE* (1982)

School was an unspeakable bore and the only thing that interested me was the teacher. The rest of my studies seemed pretty worthless. Algebra and geometry were tools of the devil, devised to make life miserable for small stupid boys.

—GROUCHO MARX, *GROUCHO AND ME* (1959)

If a man is called to be a street sweeper, he should sweep streets even as Michelangelo painted, or Beethoven composed music, or Shakespeare wrote poetry. He should sweep streets so well that all the hosts of heaven and earth will pause to say, here lived a great street sweeper who did his job well.

—MARTIN LUTHER KING, JR. (1929–1968)

The quality of a person's life is in direct proportion to their commitment to excellence, regardless of their chosen field of endeavor.

—VINCENT T. LOMBARDI (1913–1970)

School is where you go when your parents can't take you and industry can't take you.

—JOHN UPDIKE, *THE CENTAUR* (1963)

Prompt—In linear programmes a prompt usually, but not necessarily, takes the form of a verbal hint, its purpose being to help the learner to make the desired response without actually telling him or her what it is.

—*PRENTICE-HALL ENCYCLOPEDIA*
OF EDUCATION (1970)

A liberal arts education is supposed to provide you with a value system, a standard, a set of ideas, not a job.

—CAROLINE BIRD, *A CASE AGAINST COLLEGE* (1975)

When you have that seed [education], and it is flowering here, then you will keep it going all your life. But if this doesn't operate, then the world will destroy you. The world makes you what it wants you to be; a cunning animal . . .

The world is that way, deceptive, the deceiving politicians, the money-minded . . . If you are not properly educated you'll just slip into it. So what do you think is education? It is to help you fit into the mechanism of the present order, or disorder of things? Or do you think it should be something else?

—J. KRISHNAMURTI (1895–1986)

"Now then, Tommy Brown," said the teacher. "I want to set you a little problem. Suppose there were five children and their mother had only four potatoes to share between them. She wants to give each child an equal share. How would she do it?"

"Mash the potatoes," said the boy.

—*10,000 JOKES, TOASTS, AND STORIES* (1946)

The willingness to accept responsibility for one's own life is the source from which self-respect springs.

—Joan Didion (b. 1934), American novelist and social critic

A student who bought a desk dictionary from Bob Campbell's UCLA shop reported later, "It's interesting—but I wish it didn't change the subject so often."

—Bennet Cerf, *The Life of the Party* (1956)

It's your attitude and not your aptitude that determines your altitude.

—Zig Ziglar (b. 1926), American writer and motivational speaker

If education is truly liberating and genuinely makes men free, then it must provide a variety of alternatives of action, so that each man can make choices about his life and destiny.

—Gerald Gutek, *A History of the Western Educational Experience* (1994)

It's a funny thing about life; if you refuse to accept anything but the best, you very often get it.

—W. Somerset Maugham (1874–1965), English novelist

CHAPTER 7

Meditations for Teachers

"Very well," thought I, "knowledge unfits a child to be a slave."

—FREDERICK DOUGLASS, *THE LIFE AND TIMES OF FREDERICK DOUGLASS* (1881)

From the elementary classroom to the halls of higher learning, stories, quotes, and words of wisdom offer a variety of thoughts and ideas that we hope will motivate and inspire you in your quest to educate your students.

The beginning is the most important part of the work.

—PLATO (427–347 B.C.), *THE REPUBLIC*

Nothing ought to be more weighed than the nature of books recommended by a public authority. So recommended they soon form the character of the age.

—EDMUND BURKE, BRITISH POLITICAL PHILOSOPHER, IN *LETTER TO A MEMBER OF THE NATIONAL ASSEMBLY* (1791)

Above and beyond even the skill and knowledge required to work with learners, there is a need for a strong ethic of care. This, beyond all other attributes, will make the great artistic teacher. All else is technique.

—MICHAEL WODLINGER, PH.D., DIRECTOR OF RESEARCH
SERVICES AND GRADUATE STUDIES, NIPISSING
UNIVERSITY, NORTH BAY, CANADA

But the wisdom and benevolence of our fathers rested not here. They made an early provision by law that every town consisting of so many families should always be furnished with a grammar school. They made it a crime for such a town to be destitute of a grammar schoolmaster for a more than a few months and subjected it to a heavy penalty. So that the education of all ranks of people was made the care and expense of the public in a manner that I believe has been unknown to any other people, ancient or modern.

—JOHN ADAMS (1735–1826), IN *A DISSERTATION
ON THE CANON AND FEUDAL LAW* (1765)

Learning is not attained by chance, it must be sought for with ardor and attended to with diligence.

—ABIGAIL ADAMS (1744–1818), FIRST LADY TO JOHN ADAMS

The teacher is one who makes two ideas grow where only one grew before.

—ELBERT HUBBARD (1856–1915)

Education by its nature is an endless circle or spiral. It is an activity which includes science within itself. In its very process it sets more problems to be further studied, which then react into the education process to change still further, and thus demand more thought, more science, and so on, in everlasting sequence.

—JOHN DEWEY, *THE SOURCES OF A*
SCIENCE OF EDUCATION (1929)

Education does not mean teaching people what they do not know . . . It is a . . . continual and difficult work to be done with kindness, by watching, warning, by precept and by praise, but above all—by example.

—JOHN RUSKIN (1819–1900), ENGLISH
AUTHOR AND ART CRITIC

Keep away from people who try to belittle your ambitions. Small people always do that, but the really great ones make you feel that you, too, can become great.

—MARK TWAIN (1865–1910)

It is the supreme art of the teacher to awaken joy in creative expression and knowledge.

—ALBERT EINSTEIN (1879–1955)

Students are alive, and the purpose of education is to stimulate and guide their self-development. It follows as a corollary from this premise that teachers should also be alive with living thoughts.

> —ALFRED NORTH WHITEHEAD (1861–1947), PROFESSOR OF
> PHILOSOPHY AT CAMBRIDGE IN LONDON AND, LATER, AT HARVARD

Few things help an individual more than to place responsibility upon him, and to let him know that you trust him.

> —BOOKER T. WASHINGTON (1856–1915)

When we treat man as he is, we make him worse than he is; when we treat him as if he already were what he potentially could be, we make him what he should be.

> —JOHANN WOLFGANG VON GOETHE (1749–1832),
> GERMAN POET, DRAMATIST, NOVELIST, AND SCIENTIST

Responsibility educates.

> —WENDELL PHILLIPS (1811–1884), AMERICAN
> ORATOR AND SOCIAL REFORMER

Harmony cannot be brought about by unity, but unity must be attained by harmony.

> —JOHANN HEINRICH PESTALOZZI (1746–1827), SWISS EDUCATOR
> AND LEADER OF PROGRESSIVE EDUCATION MOVEMENTS IN EUROPE

Imagine how useless the most energetic work on the part of the individual teacher must be, who would fain lead a pupils back to the distant and evasive Hellenic world and the real home of culture, when in less than an hour that same pupil will have recourse to a newspaper, the latest novel, or one of those learned books, the very style of which already bears the rotting impress of modern barbaric culture.

—Friedrich Wilhelm Nietzsche (1844–1900), German philosopher, poet, and classical philologist

The true teacher defends his pupils against his own personal influence. He inspires self-distrust. He guides their eyes from himself to the spirit that quickens him. He will have no disciple.

—Amos Bronson Alcott (1799–1888), American educator and abolitionist

The system of learning which bases itself upon the actual condition of certain classes and groups of human beings is tempted to suppress a minor premise of fatal menace. It proposes that the knowledge given and the methods pursued in such institutions of learning shall be for the definite object of perpetuating present conditions or leaving their amelioration in the hands of and at the initiative of other forces and other folk.

—W. E. B. Du Bois, "The Negro College," in *The Crisis* (1933)

Instead of being shut up with one's own private feelings and sensations, [experience] signifies active and alert commerce with the world; at its height it signifies complete interpenetration of self and the world of objects and events . . . Because experience is the fulfillment of an organism in its struggles and achievements in a world of things, it is art in germ.

—JOHN DEWEY, *ART AS EXPERIENCE* (1934)

Even if you're on the right track, you'll get run over if you just sit there.

—WILL ROGERS (1879–1935)

We make a living by what we get; we make a life by what we give.

—SIR WINSTON CHURCHILL (1874–1965), PRIME MINISTER OF THE UNITED KINGDOM DURING WORLD WAR II

Another intellectual defect of almost all teaching, except the highest grade of university tuition, is that it encourages docility and the belief that definite answers are known on questions which are legitimate matters of debate.

—BERTRAND RUSSELL, *EDUCATION AND THE SOCIAL ORDER* (1932)

No experience which the child encounters becomes an integral part of his organism until he's learned it . . . The child has not reached the stage at which he is himself changed or at which he will change his behavior unless he has built up a series of concepts and associations that have resulted from vital experience.

—EDITH LEONARD, LILLIAN MILES, AND CATHERINE S. VAN DER KAR,
PROFESSORS OF EARLY CHILDHOOD EDUCATION, IN
THE CHILD AT HOME AND SCHOOL (1942)

Theories and schools, like microbes, devour one another and . . . ensure the continuity of life.

—MARCEL PROUST, *REMEMBRANCE OF THINGS PAST* (1921)

One looks back with appreciation to the brilliant teachers, but with gratitude to those who touched our human feelings. The curriculum is so much necessary raw material, but the warmth is the vital element for the growing plant and for the soul of the child.

—CARL JUNG (1875–1961), SWISS PSYCHOLOGIST
AND CONTEMPORARY OF FREUD

Oh don't the days seem lank and long
when all goes right and nothing goes wrong,
And isn't your life extremely flat
With nothing whatever to grumble at!

—W. S. GILBERT AND ARTHUR SULLIVAN, *PRINCESS IDA* (1884)

That is what learning is. You suddenly understand something you've understood all your life, but in a new way.

—DORIS LESSING (B. 1919), IRANIAN-BORN ENGLISH NOVELIST

"Here's a wonderful thing," said Mrs. Jones. "I've just been reading of a man who reached the age of forty without learning to read or write. He met a woman and, for her sake, he made a scholar of himself in two years."

"That's nothing!" replied her husband. "I know a man who was a profound scholar at forty. He met a woman, and for her sake, he made a fool of himself in two days."

—10,000 JOKES, TOASTS, AND STORIES (1946)

There was a scholar named Fressor
Whose knowledge grew lesser and lesser.
It was at last so small
He knew nothing at all
And today he's a college professor.

—BENNET CERF, THE LIFE OF THE PARTY (1956)

Teachers will never be replaced by technology. However, teachers who use technology will replace those who don't. Good teachers will include technology as part of their professional development. Excellent teachers will encourage, inspire, mentor, and help their colleagues to do the same.

—SUSAN STUCKER, FOREIGN LANGUAGE TEACHER, WINDOW ROCK, ARIZONA; RECIPIENT OF THE MILKEN NATIONAL EDUCATOR AWARD

The newest computer can merely compound, at speed, the oldest problems in relations between human beings, and in the end the communicator will be confronted with the old problem, of what to say and how to say it.

—EDWARD R. MURROW (1908–1965),
AMERICAN TELEVISION AND RADIO JOURNALIST

Computers may enhance student learning by increasing access to information, making learning more intrinsically interesting, and encouraging the learner to become self-directed. But man is a social animal; learning is a social exercise as well as an individual, private event. Successful integration of computers into the classroom may be enhanced by active collaboration among learners and between students and teachers.

—PHILIP C. ABRAMI, PROFESSOR OF PSYCHOLOGY,
UNIVERSITY OF MANITOBA, WINNIPEG, MANITOBA, CANADA

I am a special education teacher, and I had the pleasure of having an autistic child in my classroom this year. Patric was a fifth grader and this June, when he was promoted to sixth grade, he surprised me with a gift that he was eager for me to open. After I opened the present and saw that it was a beautiful table clock, Patric quickly asked if I knew why he had gotten me a clock. I replied that I didn't and to that he most lovingly answered: "Because every time you look at the clock you'll know I love you all the time."

—GABRIELA GALLARDO, SPECIAL
EDUCATION TEACHER, CALIFORNIA

It does not seem fair to ask . . . what could be more important to a teacher in his capacity as a teacher than to engage in the direct and intimate exchange of ideas with individual students? And this is what he may do when he reads seriously what students seriously write. Moreover, what is more important for the student, as a student, than to engage in the intellectual struggle to gain control of his ideas, as though writing and rewriting, he endeavors to communicate with others? Some teachers have stolen time in order to make thoughtful and sensitive comments on student papers and have been gratified to be told, "This is the first time anyone ever read my paper seriously . . ."

—Henry Gordon Hullfish, former professor of education at Ohio State University, in *Reflective Thinking: The Method of Education* (1961)

Let us think of education as the means of developing our greatest abilities, because in each of us there is a private hope and dream which, fulfilled, can be translated into benefit for everyone and greater strength for our nation.

—John F. Kennedy (1917–1963), thirty-fifth president of the United States

Children who are treated as if they are uneducable almost invariably become uneducable.

—Kenneth B. Clark, *Dark Ghetto* (1965)

Children are not simply inert vessels to be filled with the teacher's accumulated wisdom but active beings whose use of language can make a significant contribution to their learning and understanding.

—LEWIS KNOWLES, *ENCOURAGING TALK* (1983)

The goal of education is to replace an empty mind with an open mind.

—MALCOLM FORBES (1919–1990), AMERICAN PUBLISHER OF *FORBES MAGAZINE*

Top Ten Wish List:
I wish . . .
1. teachers would have respect for students.
2. teachers would realize that sometimes students act the way they do because of other outside forces.
3. all teachers taught just because they loved to do it.
4. all teachers were thinking of new and better ways to teach.
5. all teachers were inspiring students to learn.
6. teachers would understand that they should act the way they want the students to grow up to be.
7. teachers would leave politics of the school outside the classroom.
8. teachers did not hold grudges against the student just because of their parents' background.
9. teachers never picked a favorite student, but loved each one equally.
10. teachers could find a way to leave lasting memories in the students' minds.

—WHITNEY WILSON, HIGH SCHOOL SENIOR, KANSAS CITY, MISSOURI

For human minds and behavior can be controlled from without; or human minds can participate in shaping their own behavior and destiny. But the two educating processes are mutually exclusive.

—Daniel Prescott, professor of education, University of Maryland, in *The Child in the Educative Process* (1957)

The arts or skills were "liberal" because they were liberating. That is they freed their possessor from the ignorance that bound the uneducated.

—Charles Van Doren, *A History of Knowledge* (1991)

Douglas is thirty-five, mildly retarded, visually impaired, and has a mild form of cerebral palsy, which his sister at three thought might be contagious since it was called a disease. When it was determined that he would live from the severe brain injury he sustained at birth, the doctors suggested that we institutionalize him. That was not an option for our family.

So began our journey down a thoroughly uncharted road. And what a remarkable journey it has been. We didn't wait for Doug to learn. We taught him everything and he loved the discovery.

However, we never had to teach Douglas courage, for we could see it as he fought for every breath. Independence came naturally, from his first ride on a big yellow school bus to taking the subway to a work center. I can still see his pride when, on a camping trip, he spent his first night in a tent. And I remember his pride in his clever wit, when he was thirteen, after a particularly bad day, I tried to boost his trampled ego by asking, "Doug, what makes you so good looking?" and he replied, "Oh, it's just in the genes, I guess." Then he giggled.

But, most of all, I've come to admire his spirit, from taking his first communion to looking the other way when people called him retarded and forgiving them for causing him pain. We had always told him that, as in music, *retard* simply means to go slow. He found that it didn't always mean that to others. His two sisters were always there for him, one on each side, teaching and buffering him from the winds that sometimes swirled about. His father taught him to face things squarely, for that's what a man does. He was our family's cherished project.

This path we traveled was one of unconditional love and respect—respect for family, for friends, and for Doug's ever-expanding life. The front door bangs shut as this special young man leaves our world, boards a cab to the mall where he will shop for Christmas gifts for the family, for the child he sponsors in Africa, and to make his holiday contribution to the Salvation Army . . . probably all charged to his credit card, which he manages quite admirably. And my heart knows that, as it was from his very first breath, God walks beside him as He does with us all. My lesson from Doug: Against all odds, do your best and laugh along the way.

My advice: Try not to predict the future, for with faith, it will take care of itself.

—Ruth Russell, home school parent,
Fairfax County, Virginia

It certainly was the way we lived that day in Amsterdam . . . Outside the snow had stopped, but we were soon to find its equivalent nestled between the lines of the day's formal itinerary. The real serendipity, it turned out, lurked in the narrow moments between planned stops. The day's surprises, its teachable moments, were awaiting us in, of all places, boutiques and antique shops.

—THOMAS E. BARRON, "FROM THE CLASSROOMS OF STANFORD TO THE ALLEYS OF AMSTERDAM," IN *TEACHERS AS MENTORS* (1996)

I'll never forget it when a student that has tried and tested my patience looks up to me and says, "I understand." And then proceeds to demonstrate it. Nothing surpasses these moments. One of my kids watches shows like *Who Wants to Be a Millionaire?* She told me that she knew the answers to the civics questions because she learned them in my class—and then proceeded for the next ten minutes to share with the whole class and they responded positively. If that doesn't make your eyes mist, then you are in the wrong profession.

—CHARLES WOOTTEN, SEVENTH-GRADE TEACHER, PETERSBURG, VIRGINIA

We had two boys in our school this year whose dad died in a car wreck. As the official representative of the school, I went to the visitation on the night before the funeral. Although the kids are great, I really didn't know their father except for his stoic appearance at the football games and his critique of our coaches' ability.

I slid into the funeral home and immediately started sending my condolences to the people I ran into. I consoled them by gently rubbing their backs, shaking their hands and giving them my most sincere "sorry" that I could muster.

I then went to sign the "memory" book that is a permanent record of who gave of their time to observe the passing of their loved one. Not many people had made their way to sign the book yet, and I was feeling pretty good about mine being the third signature. I was pleased about this because I knew they would notice that I was there right away. I got in line to view the body. I eventually got up to the casket to view my students' dead father.

I'm not sure who the eighty-five-year-old woman was in the casket, but I was pretty sure it was not their father. I immediately felt the urge to crack up laughing but managed to hold it in. I felt empty because there was no one there I knew whom I could share my gigantic screw-up with. As I left, I wondered what the etiquette was for erasing your name from the registry!

On my way out I kept running into people in the crowded room. I thought I recognized a few of the students. I kept consoling people right out the door. I eventually made it to the right location and acted appropriately. But I couldn't wait to get to school the next day to share with my secretaries blunder number 708. My guidance counselor caught me before I could talk to anyone and said that a little girl whom she visited with first thing that morning thought that it was wonderful that I cared enough to come to her great-grandmother's funeral. I agreed. It is amazing how death seems to bring life into other relationships. I have experienced time and time again the opportunity to build a positive relationship with a child because I was there for them during a tough time.

—STEVE WOOLF, PRINCIPAL, TONGANOXIE, KANSAS;
MIDDLE SCHOOL PRINCIPAL OF THE YEAR, RECIPIENT
OF THE MILKEN NATIONAL EDUCATOR AWARD

I like bubble day where we get to make a bubble to sit in. Then we have lessons in the bubble. I think we need to make it bigger because it smells after gym when the boys take their shoes off.

JENNY A., SIXTH GRADE, PRAIRIE VILLAGE, KANSAS

Perhaps the most valuable result of all education is the ability to make yourself do the thing you have to do, when it ought to be done, whether you like it or not; it is the first lesson that ought to be learned; and however early a man's training begins, it is probably the last lesson that he learns thoroughly.

—THOMAS HENRY HUXLEY (1825–1895),
ENGLISH SCIENTIST AND AUTHOR

I always tell my students that this is the kind of thing you should understand and remember forever. It's the kind of thing that if I run into them at the mall ten years from now and I am going up the escalator and they are going down the escalator, I can shout over to them the question and they can quickly give the answers before we pass each other. Incidentally, I have done that, and it is refreshing when they get the right answer. It helps to invigorate me and keep me going after teaching for over thirty-five years.

—DIANE VAN AUSDALL, TENTH- AND TWELFTH-GRADE
TEACHER, WINDSOR, CONNECTICUT; RECIPIENT OF
THE MILKEN NATIONAL EDUCATOR AWARD

An accomplished educator is not one who has spent the most time in the classroom or won the most awards. An accomplished educator is one who has made a difference in the lives of the students. An accomplished educator helps students become better educated but also helps them become better people.

—ROSEMARY MCKNIGHT, THIRD-GRADE TEACHER, HENDERSON, TENNESSEE

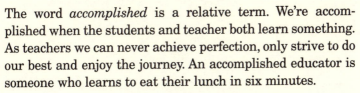

An accomplished educator is one who teaches something to all of his or her students and brings remarkable insights to some of them . . . [he or she] should instill in their students a greater appreciation for the complexity of life, and to recognize that there is always another perspective that has something to offer.

—JEFF THOMAS, FULBRIGHT SCHOLAR AND PROFESSOR OF LAW, UNIVERSITY OF MISSOURI–KANSAS CITY

The word *accomplished* is a relative term. We're accomplished when the students and teacher both learn something. As teachers we can never achieve perfection, only strive to do our best and enjoy the journey. An accomplished educator is someone who learns to eat their lunch in six minutes.

—MELINDA ABITZ, FIFTH-GRADE TEACHER, TOPEKA, KANSAS

We have more legroom when we put our supply tubs on the shelf.

—TISHA MARTIN, FOURTH GRADE, EVANSTON, ILLINOIS

What is life?

Life is a gift . . . accept it

Life is an adventure . . . dare it

Life is a mystery . . . unfold it

Life is a game . . . play it

Life is a struggle . . . face it

Life is beauty . . . praise it

Life is a puzzle . . . solve it

Life is opportunity . . . take it

Life is sorrowful . . . experience it

Life is a song . . . sing it

Life is a goal . . . achieve it

Life is a mission . . . fulfill it.

—DAVID MCNALLY, *EVEN EAGLES NEED A PUSH* (1994)

Every teacher dislikes some pupils—the cheeky lipsticked adolescent girls, the sullen, hangdog youths, the cocky vulgar little comedians, how loathsome they can be, all the more so because they do it deliberately.

—GILBERT HIGHET (1906–1978), AMERICAN EDUCATOR, AUTHOR, AND SOCIAL CRITIC

A good education and sound bringing up is of the first, middle, and last importance; and I declare to be most instrumental and conducive to virtue and happiness . . . education is of all our advantages the only one immortal and divine.

—PLUTARCH (?–120 A.D.), GREEK-BORN ROMAN HISTORIAN

No man is a good teacher unless he has feelings of warm affection towards his pupils and genuine desire to impart to them what he himself believes to be of value.

—Bertrand Russell (1872–1970), English
mathematician, logician, and philosopher

Besides pride, loyalty, discipline, heart, and mind, confidence is the key to all the locks.

—Joe Paterno (b. 1926), head football coach,
Penn State University

Student discipline—The control of student internal and external behavior to promote maximum classroom learning.

—*Encyclopedia of American Education* (1996)

The chief administrator in a school provides, at a minimum, the psychological environment in which discipline practices flourish, merely live a token existence, or die. Support for, and understanding of, the factors that are involved in classroom, building, and school community discipline are the principal's chief roles. The teacher needs to look to the principal for detailed understanding in the area.

—Richard E. Emory, "Keys to Effective Classroom Discipline,"
in *Prentice-Hall Teachers Encyclopedia* (1970)

I like it when you let us eat in the classroom.

—Jamie T., fourth grade, Portland, Oregon

CHAPTER 8

Fuel the Fire

Education is not filling a bucket, but lighting a fire.
—WILLIAM YEATS (1865–1939), IRISH PLAYWRIGHT AND POET

When students perform below their potential, they may feel frustrated. Sometimes they can meet the demands of school easily and have good grades. But they suffer from boredom. Often they become lackadaisical and indifferent. They may develop behavioral problems that result in trouble, skewed priorities, and lost opportunities. Still others may have poor grades. Their inability to solve problems may lead to a cycle of despair.

Comprehension of material, and of the ways to further their own educations, is key for all students. A teacher's positive encouragement, and sometimes gentle prodding, helps students see themselves in a brighter light—it fuels the fire to master a task and helps students see the connection between effort and accomplishment. Such thoughts are internalized and become the inner fuel that propels the student to success.

Learning without thought is labor lost; thought without learning is perilous.

—CONFUCIUS (K'UNG-FU-TZU) (551–479 B.C.),
CHINESE TEACHER, WRITER, AND PHILOSOPHER,
THE CONFUCIAN ANALECTS

A leader is at his best when people barely know he exists.

When his work is done and his goal reached, the others all say, "We did it ourselves."

—LAO-TZU (604–531 B.C.), CHINESE
PHILOSOPHER AND FOUNDER OF TAOISM

I cannot teach anybody anything. I can only make them think.

—SOCRATES (469–399 B.C.), GREEK
TEACHER AND PHILOSOPHER

If an individual knows not what harbor they seek, any wind is the right wind.

—LUCIUS ANNAEUS, AKA SENECA (4 B.C.–65 A.D.),
ROMAN DRAMATIST, PHILOSOPHER, AND STATESMAN

Much learning does not teach understanding.

—HERACLEITUS (540–470 B.C.),
GREEK PHILOSOPHER

Facts are pernicious when they do not quicken the mind that grasps them.

—GEORGE PALMER (1842–1933), AMERICAN PHILOSOPHER
AND HARVARD PROFESSOR, *THE IDEAL TEACHER*

It is not often that any man can have so much knowledge of another as to make instruction useful.

—SAMUEL JOHNSON (1709–1784), *THE RAMBLER*

None of the slaves ever had a chance to learn to read and write. Sometimes the young boys who carried the masters' children's books to and from school would ask these children to teach them to write, but as they were afraid of what their father might do they always refused. On the adjoining plantation the owner caught his son teaching a little slave boy to write. He was furious and after giving his son a very severe beating then cut off the thumb and forefinger of the slave. The only thing that were taught the slaves was the use of their hands.

—GEORGE WOMBLE, FORMER ARKANSAS SLAVE, IN *SLAVERY TIME: WHEN I WAS CHILLUN DOWN ON MARSTER'S PLANTATION* (1936)

The business of teaching is carried forward . . . because some individuals of extraordinary vitality and strength of personality engage in it and offer the fire that helps kindle the spirits of the young people whose lives they touch.

—WOODROW WILSON (1856–1921), TWENTY-EIGHTH
PRESIDENT OF THE UNITED STATES

Deciding his son needed an education and to learn some culture, a mountaineer sent him to live with a relative who was an English professor. Some months later the father decided to check on him and see how his son was doing. So he phoned the professor and said, "How's my son doing?"

The professor said, "That boy's doing fine. The fact is I'd say he's about the smartest dumb durn critter I ever seed in all my natural-born days."

—W. K. McNiell, editor, *Ozark Mountain Humor* (1989)

The whole art of teaching is only the art of awakening the natural curiosity of young minds for the purpose of satisfying it afterwards; and curiosity itself can be vivid and wholesome only in proportion as the mind is contented and happy.

—Anatole France (1844–1924), French novelist and social critic

The only weapon against bad ideas is better ideas. The source of better ideas is wisdom. The surest path to wisdom is a liberal education.

—Alfred Whitney Griswold, president of Yale University, 1950–1963

When the child doth well, let the master praise him and say, "here ye do well," for there is no such whetstone to sharpen a hand with and encourage a will to learning, as is praise.

—Roger Ascham (1515–1568), English humanist

The atmosphere at school has to be one of mutual respect and trust. These values have to be lived every day by all at school.

—ALAN GIBBY, HEAD OF INTERMEDIATE AND MIDDLE
SCHOOLS HEARTHWOOD HALL EPISCOPAL SCHOOL,
COLUMBIA, SOUTH CAROLINA

Character development—A broad area of education designed to teach students self-discipline, responsibility, and good citizenship. Character development has provoked controversies in many public school districts between parents who prefer schools to be value-neutral and those who believe schools have an obligation to shape their children's characters.

—*ENCYCLOPEDIA OF AMERICAN EDUCATION* (1996)

A student won't care how much you know until he knows how much you care.

—JAIME ESCALANTE, RETIRED BOLIVIAN-BORN
AMERICAN MATH TEACHER

Effective learning encourages the learner to use complex cognitive skills, have personal commitment to achieving them, and feel the active support of the learning community.

—PHILIP C. ABRAMI, PROFESSOR OF PSYCHOLOGY,
UNIVERSITY OF MANITOBA, WINNIPEG, MANITOBA, CANADA

The importance of parental involvement can't be underestimated. Parents should be encouraged to take an interest in their child's work. If teachers provide parents with information about what their child is learning, parents can express interest in the work. Suggesting the importance of this to parents on open house night is helpful. With the parents' interest, the child then knows they care. Successful students are often the result of teacher interest and parental involvement.

—JOHANNA WEST, ELEMENTARY SCHOOL COUNSELOR,
OVERLAND PARK, KANSAS

The only people who seem to have nothing to do with the education of the children are the parents.

—G. K. CHESTERTON (1874–1936),
ENGLISH NOVELIST AND SOCIAL CRITIC

I struggle desperately to demonstrate that the course subject matter is actually quite relevant to my bored students' lives. I try to involve the students in a running dialogue about the subject. I try to be as zany and animated as my timid soul will allow me to be.

—THAYLE ANDERSON, PROFESSOR OF ENGLISH AND
GRADUATE STUDIES DIRECTOR, MURRAY STATE
UNIVERSITY, MURRAY, KENTUCKY

Mrs. Valentine is very old and kind. She is a good teacher because she teaches me stuff that other people don't know as much. She taught me how to read. Mrs. Valentine is my friend because I have been with her three years and because she believes in me. She wants me to be really good at stuff. She is my friend because she is in my heart.

—AUSTIN, FIRST GRADE, PRAIRIE VILLAGE, KANSAS

Outstanding leaders go out of their way to boost the self-esteem in their personnel. If people believe in themselves, it's amazing what they can accomplish.

—SAM WALTON (1918–1992), FOUNDER OF WAL-MART STORES

Believe in yourself!
Have faith in your abilities!
Without a humble but reasonable confidence in your own powers you cannot be successful or happy.

—NORMAN VINCENT PEALE (1898–1993),
AMERICAN CLERGYMAN AND AUTHOR

We do not believe in ourselves until someone reveals that deep inside us is valuable, worth listening to, worthy of our trust, sacred to our touch. Once we believe in ourselves we can risk curiosity, wonder, spontaneous delight, or any experience that reveals the human experience.

—E. E. CUMMINGS (1894–1962),
AMERICAN POET AND ARTIST

A word is dead
When it is said,
Some say.
I say it just
Begins to live
That day.

—EMILY DICKINSON (1830–1886), AMERICAN POET

How does a student learn disinterested curiosity, patience, exactness, industry, and doubt . . . sensibility to small differences and the ability to recognize intellectual elegance . . . come to inherit the disposition to submit to refutation . . . learn the love of truth and justice, but learn it in a way as to escape the reproach of fanaticism? The intellectual virtues may be imparted on a teacher who really cares about them for their own sake . . . Not the cry but the rising of the wild duck impels the flock to follow him into flight.

—JOSIAH AUSPITZ, "MICHAEL OAKESHOTT,
1900–1991," IN THE AMERICAN SCHOLAR (1991)

Whether it's adding or memorizing a poem—passing a test or acing a test—the reward is reaching the goal. We used the phrase "I did it."

—MARY TEARNEY, RETIRED EDUCATOR, LEAWOOD, KANSAS

One of my students was failing three out of four core subject areas. It was February, and he was turned off by school. I read the card he filled out at the beginning of the school year and found that he loved animals and enjoyed caring for them. I told him that he could care for the animals we have in the classroom if he worked to bring his grades up. We provided tutoring, and he was able to raise his grades to Cs. We continued this the next year in seventh grade.

—RUTH RUDD, SPECIAL PROJECT EDUCATOR,
ERIE, PENNSYLVANIA

Life is like a ten-speed bike. Most of us have gears we never use.

—CHARLES SCHULZ (1922–2000),
CREATOR OF THE *PEANUTS* COMIC STRIP

I always think back about diving under my school desk when I was a very small child. I was so frightened I couldn't even look up into the sky at night. I thought a bomb was certainly coming. It is essential that schools take the safety and security of students and staff extremely serious. There need to be manuals that are jointly created and taught, but much of this preparation can happen without students there. I was once taught that the most important asset of an educator is their voice. They need to convey to the students that they need to listen to them even in a time of crisis . . .

Life is something like a trumpet. If you don't put anything into it, you don't get anything out.

—W. C. HANDY (1873–1958), MUSICIAN AND SONGWRITER

Students want to impress their classmates and will work hard to do so, especially if the work is in connection with a game or contest (or simulation). They will also work hard to appear prepared when called upon in class.

—JEFF THOMAS, PROFESSOR OF LAW,
UNIVERSITY OF MISSOURI–KANSAS CITY

Little strokes
Fell great oaks.

—BENJAMIN FRANKLIN (1706–1790)

Example is not the main thing in life—it is the only thing.

—ALBERT SCHWEITZER (1875–1965)

CHAPTER 9

Encouraging Excellence and Teamwork

A teacher's wisdom and counsel shapes our lives. They motivate us to achieve greater things than we thought possible, inspiring us to find our passion and helping us realize our potential.

As every teacher knows, underachievers may actually be bright and gifted. Their lack of "energy" or the inability to be "motivated" may come from their self-image. Teachers work with the raw material of the intellect and strive to bring it to flower through the reinforcement of students' positive aspects.

Teamwork is also important in building confidence. Each member of a great team is not necessarily a great player, but each is focused on the fact that the success of a team is dependent on the success of each player. The energy feeds on itself. A winning team will motivate individual players to achieve even greater things, for the team and for themselves.

The coaches quoted here are great teachers. They have the challenge and advantage of having to develop students physically and mentally. The coaches, with the teachers quoted here, have great advice for avoiding excess, building understanding, and bringing a motivational team spirit into the classroom.

I believe that any man's life will be filled with constant and unexpected encouragement, if he makes up his mind to do his level best each day, and as nearly as possible reaching the high water mark of pure and useful living.

—Booker T. Washington (1856–1915), former slave and founder of the Tuskegee Institute

Motivation manifests itself and becomes the basis of learning only when a child interacts with things external to himself, be these people, objects, or ideas . . . The common question "How can I motivate the children in my classroom?" is therefore a misstatement of the problem. Children are and must be motivated if they are alive. A more accurate statement of the problem would be, "How do I get particular children in particular contexts to achieve . . . ?"

A motivating classroom is people and things which challenge and support meaningful interaction and inquiry; it allows learners to completely operate and cooperate on those things that interest them.

—Walter F. Drew, Anita R. Olds, and Henry F. Olds, Jr., *Motivating Today's Students* (1974)

It's not an attribute or a skill that a teacher possesses that motivates others. It's an interest in their topic and in their students.

—Patricia Haley, retired high school English teacher, Omaha, Nebraska

We take the time to listen to the children, to observe them, talk with them, and help with those problems. We're just now learning what is important to us as teachers—helping children understand that what they think, they feel, and what they do is important.

—LYNN MCCARROLL, CHRIS O'CONNOR, AND MARION MORRISEY,
"LEARNING IS A BACK-AND-FORTH PROCESS," IN
MOTIVATING TODAY'S STUDENTS (1974)

Most students work hard to please the adults in their lives
. . . the children are seeking love and approval.

—CINDI HARRISON, PRINCIPAL, DALLAS, TEXAS

One of the biggest motivators is the feeling of success, so if you can get them to sense they are doing the right thing— oftentimes they just take off . . .

With adults I give small jobs and then put deadlines on them. I ask them to come back at a specific time with X accomplished. Follow up! Many adults have trouble with deadlines and motivation. It is essential that someone keep reminding them of the purpose of their position and hopefully that will eventually become internal to their drive. Let them feel success in small bites and then give them larger tasks to accomplish that show them that they are the only thing holding themselves back.

—DR. JO CAMPBELL, ASSISTANT SUPERINTENDENT OF
ELEMENTARY SCHOOLS, COUNCIL BLUFFS, IOWA; RECIPIENT
OF THE MILKEN NATIONAL EDUCATOR AWARD

The students must feel that the teacher cares about them as people. Beyond that I think that to motivate students a teacher has to show them something that they haven't seen before—an idea, a vision of what could be, something to dream about.

—FRANCES MCLEAN COLEMAN, HIGH SCHOOL SCIENCE TEACHER, ACKERMAN, MISSISSIPPI; ALBERT EINSTEIN DISTINGUISHED EDUCATOR FELLOW; RECIPIENT OF THE MILKEN NATIONAL EDUCATOR AWARD

As a teacher, the most important thing I am concerned with is helping a few students see how great their potential is, and working towards that potential. It makes no difference whether the student becomes a scientist, businessman, or mechanic, just so he or she sees growth. Should the student become tired in what they are doing, I would hope the teacher would have the gumption to make changes that would motivate and inspire the student's learning style.

—LAVOIR BANKS, RETIRED PROFESSOR OF CHEMISTRY, BRIGHAM YOUNG UNIVERSITY, OGDEN, UTAH

I believe athletics is part of an education of a young person, as the Greeks and the English schoolmaster believed; and I believe athletics teaches lessons valuable to the individual in ways nothing else can.

—A. BARTLETT GIAMATTI, *A FREE AND ORDERED SPACE* (1988)

I believe in the power of a little friendly competition. Mastering grammar and sentence structure solely on paper can drive unmotivated individuals right out the door. Instead, I set up a mock auction, for example: I pulled random sentences from everyone's papers, typed them as is (no names), and gave everyone a copy. In groups, they had to decide which, if any, were grammatically correct. Each group received an imaginary pot of $5,000 that they then used to bid on correct sentences. The winner was the group with the most correct sentences and the most money left. In activities like this, students were always interested to see their own work used in class and were motivated to find others' mistakes. Even the guy who always slouched in the back of the room got into seeing his work compared to others.

—CHRISTI CLEMONS HOFFMAN, ENGLISH TEACHER,
FORMERLY OF ECOLE ZARADI, GENEVA, SWITZERLAND

A great coach is also a great teacher. They're consistent and disciplined. They know that the student athlete will perform at the highest level if the student knows the coach or teacher really cares for them.

—JIM BENNICK, HEAD FOOTBALL COACH,
WISCONSIN RAPIDS, WISCONSIN

I used to think you had to be on the winner's podium to be considered a success. Now I realize it is all about the journey. The paycheck for the coach is seeing a player improve and developing a lifelong relationship with him and his parents.

The journey begins by developing a relationship with a player. A player will improve if the coach is willing to work hard at developing a common language that the two of you understand. A coach has to learn to listen and pay attention to what his players are saying. When I was the coach at West Point, I learned that the journey is not about where you finish, it's where you take them.

The key to coaching is listening. Learn what drives them. Be prepared to listen to their personal problems and concerns. Find out about their families. Be there when the player needs you. Over time your players will figure out that it is almost impossible to fool you because you know all about them. A coach who knows his players will recognize when things aren't quite right. That is when a coach is needed and can help. It is up to me to help each player with his journey.

—PAUL ASSAIANTE, HEAD COACH FOR MEN'S TENNIS/MEN'S SQUASH AT TRINITY COLLEGE, HARTFORD, CONNECTICUT, AND HEAD COACH OF THE 2000 U.S. PAN AMERICAN GAMES TEAM AND 2001 U.S. WORLD CHAMPIONSHIP TEAM

It doesn't take much to motivate your players if you all are on the same page, if you have the same goals and aspirations. If your players believe in you as a coach and what you are trying to do, they will be easily motivated or inspired by your words, goals, and dreams . . . If the players do not respect their coach, there is nothing he or she can say to motivate or inspire them.

A coach, like the teacher in the classroom, needs to be creative. You must put in new plays, new drills, a different pregame speech or routine. Try yelling when the team thinks you'll be positive and be encouraging when they're expecting a blow-up.

—JEFF SPEEDY B.PE., M.ED., UNIVERSITY OF THE COLLEGE OF THE CARIBOO, BRITISH COLUMBIA

We are not sports franchises. I don't want to turn off the game; I just want to turn down the volume.

—MYLES BRAND, INDIANA UNIVERSITY PRESIDENT, SPEAKING ON EDUCATION REFORM BEFORE A NATIONALLY TELEVISED AUDIENCE AT THE NATIONAL PRESS CLUB IN WASHINGTON, D.C. (2001)

One skill that is most likely to serve a coach well in keeping an athlete motivated is always being an educator.

—MARIAN JONES, SPEECH AND LANGUAGE INSTRUCTOR, WATKINSVILLE, GEORGIA

The most significant factor in motivating athletes is showing them that you care about them as people in their individual, everyday lives. A coach cannot talk to athletes only in season and only about the sport that he or she coaches and be successful for very long. Coaches that sincerely care about athletes and talk with them about other things in their lives make a connection with kids [athletes]. That connection is essential to success.

—JAMES AND DAWN KUCHTA. JAMES KUCHTA WAS AN ALL-AMERICAN SMALL-COLLEGE FOOTBALL ATHLETE AND HAS BEEN A COACH FOR ALMOST TWENTY YEARS. DAWN KUCHTA WAS AN ALL-AMERICAN GYMNAST AND IS CURRENTLY COACHING.

I like to use stories to get across ideas and contextual points. It tends to "fire up"' the student's imagination. Also, by engaging the students in class discussions, they come to realize that most learning occurs outside the classroom. Having a sense of humor certainly doesn't hurt either!

—CHRISTINE BUTTERILL, PH.D., DEAN OF STUDENTS,
ST. PAUL'S COLLEGE, WINNIPEG, MANITOBA, CANADA

Always be passionate about your team's goals. Be a positive role model towards those goals. "Walk the walk, and talk the talk." Understand that you have to treat each athlete differently. Some need inspiration, attention, and intensity. Some need a calming influence.

—RICK BEVIS, MALASPINA UNIVERSITY-COLLEGE, BRITISH
COLUMBIA, HEAD COACH WOMEN'S VOLLEYBALL

Students know if you're a fair person. They watch everything you do. They know if you're real or a fake. They know if you treat everyone fairly. You can get students to do anything for you if they trust you and know you care about them.

—SARA KINNEY, COACH AND TEACHER FOR MORE THAN
TWENTY-FIVE YEARS, CHILLICOTHE, ILLINOIS

Have great passion for and great desire to serve the athletes as both people and athletes.

—KARLA WOLTERS, HEAD COACH FOR WOMEN'S SOFTBALL,
HOPE COLLEGE, HOLLAND, MICHIGAN

This is my thirty-third year of coaching and teaching physical education. Last year I was inducted into the Wisconsin Football High School Coaches Hall of Fame. The first attribute a coach must have is that he must care about his athletes as individual people and strive to make them better not only athletically but more importantly a better person. He does this by teaching character, leadership, and self-discipline and always striving to improve the athlete's self-image. It takes ten positives to overcome one negative comment in a young person's life.

The second attribute is that the coach must have a positive mental attitude and he must teach this to his athletes. Ninety percent of success is due to a positive mental attitude that will not accept defeat. Ninety percent of failure is not due to being defeated but due to our giving up and quitting.

The most important skill a coach can have to keep his athletes motivated is to recognize that each one is different. Some you have to kick in the rear end and others need a pat on the back and a word of encouragement. Some are self-motivators and others you have to get right in their face. Top this off with always being positive and always encouraging.

If you truly care about kids and are a positive encourager the players will be on your side and the wins will take care of themselves.

—Robert McLeod, Ashland, Wisconsin

If athletes rather than scholars are seen as representative of educational institutions, the probable reason is that sports are a lowest common denominator, a signifier whose significance anyone can understand.

—Allen Guttman, *A Whole New Ballgame* (1988)

The mere athlete becomes too much of a savage.

—PLATO (427–347 B.C.)

A college which is interested in producing professional athletes is not an educational institution.

—ROBERT MAYNARD HUTCHINS, PRESIDENT OF THE
UNIVERSITY OF CHICAGO, 1945–1951

I had my heart ripped out a little bit this morning. We had an eighth-grade young man who was one of our major pain-in-the-rears last year. He would be sent to the office for discipline at least every couple of weeks and was not a very pleasant person to be around. Last year we found out that this young man was living out of his family's car with his mom, dad, and brother. We had been concerned for the social, mental, and physical health of this kid for quite a while.

This year we were expecting the worst from him but we were shocked. For some reason he stayed out of trouble, treated people with kindness and respect, and excelled academically. He had gone from failing nearly every class to being on the honor roll!

I believe that much of his turnaround had come through his involvement this year in athletics. He had great success in football and wrestling. He was a large kid, which helped him in football and qualified him to be on our heavyweight wrestling team.

It had worked out that I was the administrator on duty this year for every wrestling match home and away. The benefits of spending that much time with one sport come out in knowing the participants and watching them progress throughout the season.

We had fairly close meets that came down to the final wrestle to determine who would have the most points to win the meet. What pressure! I could see the stress on his face every time he stepped on the mat. Knowing the kid made my gut tie up in knots as well. I had seen him wrestle some tough matches, but he had not been beat.

I had made a practice of leaving the stands after he wrestled to see him. We more or less had a ritual. I gave him a big hug and told him how proud I was of him. He then replied, "Thank you, sir." I always got a "Thank you, sir" with a big smile.

The last meet we had I was there the whole time and worked to supervise the crowd. I cheered loud the whole match. Our young man won his bout, and I got busy supervising the crowd as they left. I did not get to my ritual of giving him a hug and telling him how proud I was of him.

The next morning he came into my office and asked if I was going to come to his wrestling match. I assured him that I would not miss it. He then asked me why I had not been at his last match. I was shocked. I had been there and cheered loudly. I told him I was there and he had done a great job. He still looked a little dejected and asked, "Why didn't you come down to see me after my match?"

I didn't realize how important that brief amount of time of caring, physical contact, and words of affirmation were to him. I prayed that I not miss out on such opportunities to lift kids up again. I also prayed that I be insightful enough to know when those moments were.

Guess whose match I did not miss that afternoon!

—STEVE WOOLF, PRINCIPAL, TONGANOXIE, KANSAS; MIDDLE SCHOOL PRINCIPAL OF THE YEAR, RECIPIENT OF THE MILKEN NATIONAL EDUCATOR AWARD

I want parents to know that we are a team—student, teacher, parent. The student is the star player. So many times it appears that we are on two separate teams. However, we really both have the same goal in mind—to do what is best for their child.

—ANGIE BESENDORFER, PRINCIPAL, CARTHAGE, MISSOURI

When cooperative learning classes are working well, it's quite common to read comments such as, "I'm surprised how much we learned about teamwork, in addition to learning the course material."

—KARL SMITH-MORSE, DIRECTOR OF UNDERGRADUATE
STUDIES FOR CIVIL ENGINEERING, UNIVERSITY
OF MINNESOTA AT MINNEAPOLIS

My goal is to motivate and excite students with imaginative group projects that will challenge them to be more creative, passionate thinkers and doers. The creative energy is definitely felt when entering my classroom, because I set high expectations for quality work and personal presentations.

—MADONNA HANNA, HIGH SCHOOL FASHION-MARKETING
INSTRUCTOR, BREMERTON, WASHINGTON; RECIPIENT
OF THE MILKEN NATIONAL EDUCATOR AWARD

In today's world, the ability to cooperate and work with a team is nearly as important as the skills one possesses.

—STEWART ELLIOTT, INVESTMENT BANKER,
HAT CREEK PARTNERS, DALLAS, TEXAS

Teachers must not overlook the matter of teamwork. Frequently the school presents a united approach to discipline. Remember to be willing to play your part on that team approach.

—RICHARD E. EMORY, "KEYS TO EFFECTIVE CLASSROOM DISCIPLINE," *PRENTICE-HALL TEACHERS ENCYCLOPEDIA* (1970)

I like to put four or five students in a group, give them the topic, and let them collaborate. Collaborative learning gives the students the opportunity to work together in a cooperative environment. They discuss among themselves (typically without my intervention) the problems or issues to be solved. This allows them to consider the viewpoint of each other, develop a sense of teamwork, and use their critical thinking skills at the same time.

—JENNIE TUSHER, SIXTH-GRADE TEACHER, BONNER SPRINGS, KANSAS

CHAPTER 10

Everyday Tips for the Classroom

I have found the best way to give advice to your children is to find out what they want and then advise them to do it.

—HARRY S. TRUMAN, PRESIDENT OF THE
UNITED STATES, 1945–1953

Some simple suggestions can make the classroom experience more productive and enjoyable. Though these "tips" don't represent an exhaustive list, they provide a good starting point: Refresh yourself each day. Think of ways to add variety to the classroom experience.

There can be no education without leisure, and without leisure education is worthless.

—SARAH JOSEPHA HALE (1788–1879),
AMERICAN NOVELIST AND EDITOR

I can't tell if a straw ever saved a drowning man, but I know that a mere glance is enough to make despair pause.

—Joseph Conrad (1857–1927), English novelist

The art of teaching is the art of self-discovery.

—Mark Van Doren (1894–1972), American poet, teacher, and writer of plays, essays, and children's books

Habits are formed by the repetition of particular acts. They are strengthened by an increase in the number of repeated acts. Habits are also weakened or broken, and contrary habits are formed by the repetition of contrary acts.

—Mortimer Adler (b. 1902)

In all the work at Tuskegee Institute I have lost no opportunity to impress upon our teachers the importance of having their students study, analyze, and compare actual things, and to use what they have learned in the schoolroom and in the textbook to enable them to observe, think about, and deal with the objects and situations of actual life . . .

My experience has taught me that the surest way to success in education, and in any other line for that matter, is to stick close to the common and familiar things—things that concern the common greater part of the people the greater part of the time. I want to see education as common as grass, and free for all as the sunshine.

—Booker T. Washington,
My Larger Education (1911)

Public speaking and dramatics appeal to many students as an outlet, but the high school newspaper seems to attract a far greater number. Perhaps it is the glamour of newspaper work which appeals to these students, or it may be the natural desire to delve into other people's activities, to put the same into written expression and to see it in print . . .

The school newspaper which represents a true interpretation of school and community life is read not only by students but also by advertising patrons, parents, and others interested in "what's going on" in the school. The adult readers often hold more belief in items appearing in the school paper than those appearing in the public press . . .

The annual or yearbook is a school history or memory book published by some particular class . . . and contains a résumé of high spots of the school year and pictures of activities . . . The value of high school formation is looked upon from the angles of both the English class and professional newspaper training.

—H. S. HEPNER, *THE HIGH SCHOOL JOURNALIST* (1936)

It is possible for any school to start a magazine and to produce it regularly at little cost. It will, of course, be a simple affair but the entire process can be carried out in the classroom and its educational value may be considerable.

—MELVILLE HARDIMENT, *MAGAZINE PRODUCTION FOR SCHOOLS* (1963)

I find television very educational. Every time someone switches it on I go into another room and read a good book.

—GROUCHO MARX (1890–1977)

Museums, especially natural science museums, are a tool for teachers to use for bringing hard to describe concepts required by classic curriculum to life for students. The age and biodiversity of our earth, for instance, or size and anatomy of a dinosaur, or today's butterfly—even their existence is hard to grasp without actually seeing a 100 million-year-old fossil of one standing over you, or watching the metamorphosis of a pupa into artful wings as an example of the long evolution of nature's wonderful and diverse array of living creatures. No teacher or book alone can have as much impact as the real thing on children's learning!

—ROBERT H. TOWNSEND, EXECUTIVE DIRECTOR, DALLAS MUSEUM OF NATURAL HISTORY, DALLAS, TEXAS

Make the beginning of each study unit like it was the first day of school.

—NICK DIFLAVIO, EDUCATIONAL INTERNET PROVIDER

Being creative can mean a lot of things. It can be as simple as using visuals to describe the subject. I'd been on an African safari and one of the best classes I had was our study of the continents. Of course Africa was the students' favorite because of the pictures and artifacts I brought back from the trip.

—BELINDA STUART, EIGHTH-GRADE TEACHER, DALLAS, TEXAS

What should be the concern of a teacher as he reads the written work of students? There is no simple answer to this question. The student should be helped to get control of a sentence. He should learn the value of a crisp sentence or, indeed, of a complex one . . . He should develop a respect for words as tools of thinking; hence, he should treat them with the same care that a tool deserves . . .

A sensitive teacher will read each paper . . . in relation to the student who wrote it. If a student has a tough hide, the marginal notations will be sharp. If a student has been timid about writing because of insecurity bred from lack of experience, a gentle marginal touch, rather than the use of a spur, will be indicated.

—HENRY GORDON HULLFISH, *REFLECTIVE THINKING: THE METHOD OF EDUCATION* (1961)

Children love color, but they thrive on order. They appreciate beauty, but they are distracted and bothered by busyness. They feel comfortable and secure in a simple, quiet atmosphere, but they need freedom of movement and challenging, changing eye-catching arrangements . . .

Individual abilities and interests of children vary widely. Care should be taken to provide a classroom arrangement that will permit children to make use of their individual abilities by exploring fields of interest.

—BETTY LOU PAGEL, COORDINATOR OF ELEMENTARY GRADES IN THE CHEYENNE, WYOMING, ELEMENTARY SCHOOLS, IN *INCREASING THE HOLDING POWER OF THE CLASSROOM* (1966)

Periods of tranquility are seldom prolific of creative achievement. Mankind has to be stirred up.

—ALFRED NORTH WHITEHEAD (1861–1947)

I don't have much of a philosophical bent, so my advice about teaching and learning are pretty much on the pragmatic side: Quit whining, go to work, and accomplish something! Self-esteem is something that we earn, not something that we are born with or that is bestowed on us by someone else. When I'm in doubt, I stop whining, go to work, and accomplish something. Self-doubt disappears.

—RAYMOND BAUER, PROFESSOR OF MARINE BIOLOGY, UNIVERSITY OF LOUISIANA AT LAFAYETTE

I try to move around the classroom. My desk is only a place to organize and collect my paperwork. The days of sitting behind the desk are long gone. Moving through the classroom shows the students that you're interested and also watching what they're doing.

—GINNY GLEN, EIGHTH-GRADE SOCIAL STUDIES TEACHER, TALLAHASSEE, FLORIDA

Books are the least important apparatus in school. All a child needs is the three Rs; the rest should be tools and clay and sports and theatre and paint and freedom.

—A. S. NIELL, *SUMMERHILL* (1969)

One of the best things I do as a professional working in the public schools is to make home visits. I don't do it with every student but only those who are having difficulties. It is amazing the insights you gain from stepping into a student's world. The problems they display in school can almost always be traced to their home environment. Once a teacher has a better understanding of the home, he or she is better able to develop strategies to deal with the problem.

—WENDY NEIHART, SCHOOL CLINICAL PSYCHOLOGIST,
KANSAS CITY, KANSAS

Use real life analogies.

—JOSHUA H., ELEVENTH GRADE, DULUTH, MINNESOTA

The three Rs of our school system must be supported by the three Ts—teachers who are superior, techniques of instruction that are modern, and thinking about education which places it first in all our plans and hopes.

—LYNDON BAINES JOHNSON, THIRTY-SIXTH PRESIDENT
OF THE UNITED STATES, MESSAGE TO CONGRESS (1965)

A workshop classroom operates a little like an art studio. After a short demonstration, students paint as their teacher circulates among them to help. The students learn to paint as they paint. In reading and writing workshops, students learn to read and write as they read and write. This independent reading and writing is one essential element of a workshop classroom . . .

I became acquainted with them in all their uniqueness. To begin, I wrote a diary schedule on a poster. I gave an overview of the day—brief explanations of what to do at a particular time—and explained that it was all right if the children did not understand completely what to do. Every time we began a new activity, I explained . . .

As I taught procedures and observed the children's responses I took notes. The notes helped me decide what to do next.

—CATHY ROLLER, *VARIABILITY, NOT DISABILITY* (1996)

I try to remain positive and encourage my students to do the same. Sometimes I introduce a little levity or something "slightly offbeat." I like to tease and cajole them. More than anything, a smile goes a long way. After I get to know my students, and they know me, I can introduce an atmosphere of heightened anticipation of what is to come in the lesson. This helps to set the tone and create a productive environment. Above all, I like my students and they know it.

—DIANE VAN AUSDALL, TENTH- AND TWELFTH-GRADE TEACHER, WINDSOR, CONNECTICUT; RECIPIENT OF THE MILKEN NATIONAL EDUCATOR AWARD

Teachers generally have insisted that it is more economical to learn by authority. It now seems that many important things, though not all, can be learned more effectively and economically in creative ways rather than by authority.

—PAUL E. TORRANCE, *ENCOURAGING CREATIVITY* (1963)

Time invested in getting to know pupils, their problems, and parents and purposes, yields a rich harvest later. And the sooner you get to know them, the better, for knowing them will help you to plan the instructional program for the group (and to provide diverse programs for the individuals who make up the group). Knowing them will help to establish the warm personal teacher-pupil relationship so necessary to a child's feeling of security and belonging.

—JAMES M. CRONIN, "IMPROVING YOUR CLASSROOM PRODUCTIVITY," IN *PRENTICE-HALL TEACHERS ENCYCLOPEDIA* (1970)

Nature hikes during the spring and summer feature wild-flower, tree, and plant identification, insect and fossil collecting, and many other interesting activities. Fall hikes feature trees in their autumn splendor of reds, browns, golds, and greens. Many city children seldom get an opportunity to enjoy this spectacle of nature, except on an outing of this type.

—NORMAN SOMMERS, PRINCIPAL, GREENWICH, OHIO, IN *PRENTICE-HALL TEACHERS ENCYCLOPEDIA* (1970)

Reading aloud, when done well, provides the opportunity to share the pleasure of the literature, and also to sense and respond to the rhythm, style, and meaning of the author's words . . . Storytelling is a demanding art. It is also sadly neglected in today's schools. With the right combination of story time, place, and audience, you will see the almost magical effect of the story on the listening audience. The results will be well worth your time and effort.

—*PRENTICE-HALL TEACHERS ENCYCLOPEDIA* (1970)

Allow students to use their senses and discover how to "do" science as opposed to "reading about" science. Give them the opportunity to release their natural curiosities in order to explore and discover basic science concepts in a user-friendly but stimulating environment. Have "ready made" or "improvised" materials available so students of varied abilities and attention spans can latch onto simple or difficult concepts that tend to escape them during those crucial adolescence years. Be ever mindful of an old Chinese proverb that says, "I see and I forget, I hear and I remember, I do and I understand." This approach follows the basic philosophy that science is a process in which students are active participants. Prepare the meal, set the table, and allow your students to dine until their hearts are content.

—ABRAHAM FUNCHESS, SIXTH-GRADE GENERAL SCIENCE TEACHER, ST. MATTHEWS, SOUTH CAROLINA; RECIPIENT OF THE MILKEN NATIONAL EDUCATOR AWARD

Using stories is a great way of instilling the subject matter into the student's mind. Have them share their own stories. Personal stories have a way of imprinting the topic or subject in a way facts and figures don't.

—WILLIAM BURK, FIFTH-GRADE TEACHER, FORT WAYNE, INDIANA

Regularly post assignments in the same place or via the same method each day. Don't count solely on auditory instructions or a handout as adequate notice.

—GENE BRAND, SIXTH-GRADE TEACHER, DETROIT, MICHIGAN

Read with expression to the children. Don't be their mom.

—NETTY S., THIRD GRADE, FORT COLLINS, COLORADO

Role playing, like telling stories, brings to life the topic. I've had students recite in front of the class the quotes of famous people. If they wish, they can dress up like the character. I've had Ben Franklin, George Washington, famous athletes, and a variety of others come to my class. The students love it and take away more from the lesson.

—JAMES BURNS, HIGH SCHOOL HISTORY TEACHER,
SILVER SPRING, MARYLAND

By giving older children some responsibility for helping others—especially younger children—the intermediate generation of youth could gain a sense of purpose and useful participation all too often lacking in their lives . . .

Preliminary results reported from tutoring programs have indicated strongly that when a child helps teach [tutor] another child in school, both the older and the younger may profit in terms of better academic achievement and improved personal-social behavior.

—VERNON ALLEN, *CHILDREN AS TEACHERS* (1976)

The only good advice is a good example.

—OSSIE DAVIS (B. 1917), AMERICAN ACTOR

Active listening is listening with the intent to understand the questions, needs, or ideas of the students, while passive listening is waiting for the student to finish talking so you can respond. Active listening engages while passive listening ignores.

—SHERRY MICHAELS, MIDDLE SCHOOL COUNSELOR,
PHILADELPHIA, PENNSYLVANIA

I remember one school where the teacher wanted the children to "become more responsible" and along with this hoped that the mothers would become more responsible too. The teacher noted that the children didn't do their homework and frequently didn't have milk in their lunches, or in some way, demonstrated irresponsibility on the part of students and mothers.

The teacher agreed that the children keep a diary of daily activity . . . When the diaries were read she discovered to her surprise and horror that these children who she had seen as irresponsible were in fact overwhelmed with duties and tasks and chores at home—where everyone, in fact, was overworked, and where, for example, mothers didn't have milk on hand because there was no refrigeration to keep it cold . . . She began to change entirely her view of what might be needed.

—ELIZABETH HALL BRADY, "HILDA TABA:
THE CONGRUITY OF PROFESSING AND DOING,"
IN *TEACHERS AS MENTORS* (1996)

Asking open-ended questions is a great way to offer students a way to think for themselves. Questions with more than one answer give the students an opportunity to think critically at any level. For example, in a class on Native American Indians, I asked the question "What kind of homes or dwellings did the Native American Indians live in?" The students realized that depending on geographical location, Native Americans lived in a variety of dwellings. From homes on stilts in the Southeast and adobe dwellings in the Southwest to moveable teepees on the plains.

—DENNY JOHNSON, FORMER ELEMENTARY TEACHER,
SANTA FE, NEW MEXICO

Only by helping my kids explore and accept their own potential and limitations will they not have to rely so much on mine. They will be more capable of making their own choices and dealing with their own problems . . .

I think it unfair to require a kid to do something without any choice, and I think it is equally unfair to tell a kid he can choose to do anything he wants. Expecting him to make all his own choices is a subtle way of fooling him, pretending you don't have expectations. I feel I must be as clear as possible with the kids about whatever expectations I have.

—BOBBI SHAW, "MOTIVATION IS MORE THAN RAZZLE-DAZZLE
SHOWMANSHIP," IN *MOTIVATING TODAY'S STUDENTS* (1974)

An individual can learn through the process of teaching someone else. Learning through teaching can be an important way to understand new material. In preparing to teach, one must develop example, analogies, illustrations, and applications in order to help the learner grasp the material. In so doing, the teacher himself improves the understanding of the material . . . Children should have the opportunity to learn through teaching other children.

—VICTOR G. CICIRELLI, PURDUE UNIVERSITY PROFESSOR OF EDUCATION, "SIBLINGS TEACHING SIBLINGS," IN *CHILDREN AS TEACHERS* (1976)

I find that using "real" materials in the classroom reinforces the lessons I'm trying to teach. Whether it's a study about how glass is made (where I use sand and other materials) or walking through a park and picking up the leaves from different trees, when students can smell, touch, and feel their subject, they learn better.

—KELLY JAMES, SECOND-GRADE TEACHER, PORTLAND, OREGON

They [students] have not been taught to use a library. I sense that most of them have been conditioned and programmed to be conveniently pumped into the system of corporate America.

—HELEN CALDICOTT, *IF YOU LOVE THIS PLANET* (1992)

As the saying goes, "You're never too old to learn." It's true. One of the ways that I stay sharp in the classroom is by attending workshops, reading books and articles, and discussing with other teachers the issues that affect me. I recently attended a workshop on ESL [English as a second language]. What I learned in the four-hour seminar was worth more than the cost of the seminar.

—TRACEY WILCOX, NINTH-GRADE TEACHER, PLANO, TEXAS

Holding yourself accountable is as important as anything you'll do as an educator. By holding yourself accountable to deadlines, class preparation, understanding of the subject matter, you will instill in your students a good model for living the same way. The old saying "Do what I say, not as I do" is never more applicable than in the classroom.

—ANGIE JENKINS, EIGHTH-GRADE MATH TEACHER, GLENDALE, CALIFORNIA

Teaching is a process that continues well after your first, third, or twentieth year. It's what keeps it interesting. Teachers must be thinkers and decision makers who take full responsibility for their classrooms and students. It's a continual search for knowledge. Teaching relies on the judgment of its "individual practitioners"—it's called the "art of teaching."

—KATHLEEN LANGE, FIFTH-GRADE TEACHER, CLARKSVILLE, TENNESSEE; RECIPIENT OF THE MILKEN NATIONAL EDUCATOR AWARD; PHI DELTA KAPPA OUTSTANDING EDUCATOR

As most of us know, the Internet is an amazing technology. A lot of people (yes, even teachers) are hesitant to use it. I have to admit that my students know more about it than I do. But the fact is that the Internet is changing the way we do everything. I've used it to retrieve lesson plans, create my own, and just generally find out about topics that are hard to find anywhere else. As they say, the future is now. Take the plunge and utilize this great teaching tool. It's here to stay!

—EDWARD MCPHAIL, SIXTH-GRADE TEACHER, LAKE PLACID, NEW YORK

Recognize that everyone has weaknesses and that they need to deal with them, learn from them, and move on to the next step. Some adults, as with students, have a hard time seeing that they do anything wrong, and others see nothing but fault in everything they do. Take small steps by pointing out their troubles in a supportive and dignified way allowing them to learn from their mistakes and move on.

—DR. JO CAMPBELL, ASSISTANT SUPERINTENDENT OF
ELEMENTARY SCHOOLS, COUNCIL BLUFFS, IOWA;
RECIPIENT OF THE MILKEN NATIONAL EDUCATOR AWARD

One thing I do as a teacher is to make my classroom a place where mathematics is honored. When students walk into my room, they see a rich mathematical place with posters of people who do mathematics, activity centers where they can play with soma cubes or tangrams, problems of the day, and daily activity sets. I wear math ties upon occasion and share with them my enthusiasm about mathematics. I consider myself a salesman for mathematics and strive every day to "sell" my students on the joys of math. "A day without math is a day without sunshine!" is a phrase they often hear from me because I believe that they shouldn't leave school without it.

—JOHN D. PUTNAM, RETIRED SEVENTH- THROUGH
NINTH-GRADE MATH TEACHER; RECIPIENT OF
THE MILKEN NATIONAL EDUCATOR AWARD

I have found that having a file folder for each subject and a check-off sheet for each assignment helps students turn their work in on time. Having a personal assignment planner also helps the individual complete the work that needs to be done.

—NANCY CHAPIN, FIFTH-GRADE TEACHER, DENVER, COLORADO

Parents are and can become more effective teachers of their children; they can take an active role in the development of planned home learning activities for their youngsters. Parents working with other parents, home visitors, and professionals strengthen the child's entire home/school learning experiences.

—ATHOL PACKER, STEVE HOFFMAN, BETTY BOZLER, AND NANCY BEAR, *HOME LEARNING ACTIVITIES FOR CHILDREN* (1976)

The importance of parental involvement can't be forgotten. Students fare much better when they know that their parents are concerned and care about behavior and grades. I make sure parents are aware of their students' progress by sending home midquarter updates, which the parent is asked to sign. The student is responsible for returning the report to me signed. I provide an opportunity for the parents to ask questions or make comments. I also send home a weekly checklist on Friday indicating that week's behavior, assignments on time and late, a blurb on what we are doing in class, etc.

—THOMAS PETRIE, NINTH-GRADE SCIENCE TEACHER, HAWTHORNE, CALIFORNIA

To My Students' Parents:

I am looking forward to working with your child this year. Let's begin the school year in the spirit of partnership and cooperation. I'll believe half of what I hear about you if you believe half of what you hear about me! From time to time we will need to speak honestly and openly about your child. There are appropriate times to do this. So I thought I would take this opportunity to let you know how I work.

My time just before and just after the bell rings is devoted to my students. Stopping to talk at the door would be like hosting a birthday party and a parent catches you to schedule a play date while your guests are still there and needing your attention. My time belongs to my students as long as they are in my classroom. Please e-mail or leave me a voice message on my school phone. We can plan to talk. There may be reasons behind the problems and together we can work them through.

As certain as the morning dawn returns, there will be homework! Studying at home provides an opportunity for your student to learn responsibility and take ownership of his own education. This is also a time for introspection. Can they follow instructions and do it on their own? To make this experience more inviting, set aside a special place to study, equipped with the school supplies they may need. Having paper, pencils, colors, etc., in one place and having a set time to do this work makes the experience less stressful for all. Routines are good. But routines only work when the right study atmosphere is set for the student beforehand.

—SUZANNE PALMER, SIXTH-GRADE TEACHER,
ORLANDO, FLORIDA

CHAPTER 11

When the Going Gets Tough

Be swift to hear, slow to speak, slow to wrath.

—JAMES 1:19

Even the best-run classrooms don't run perfectly every day. In fact, few classrooms run on all cylinders all of the time. Teaching is a challenging profession that requires a mixture of hope, faith, and love and more than a few techniques to keep students on the long road to discovery. What are some things you can do to stay sane when the going gets tough?

The following thoughts and ideas will help you gain a little perspective. Here is criticism that will help you gain the sense of humor that Mark Twain, Henny Youngman, and Dr. Gary Fine of the University of Minnesota recommend to carry you through rough waters. Others let you know you are not alone when the going gets tough. And there are some good ideas for lifting yourself and your students out of the doldrums.

Be patient, if they don't get it the first time, just be patient.

—LAUREL F., THIRD GRADE,
FORT COLLINS, COLORADO

Travel, in the younger sort, is a part of education; in the elder, a part of experience.

—FRANCIS BACON (1561–1626), ENGLISH
PHILOSOPHER, SCIENTIST, AND STATESMAN

The vanity of teaching often tempts man to forget he is a blockhead.

—GEORGE SAVILE (1633–1695), MEMBER OF
THE BRITISH HOUSE OF LORDS

Everybody who is incapable of learning had taken to teaching—that is really what our enthusiasm for education has come to.

—OSCAR WILDE, *THE DECAY OF LYING* (1889)

Art is a form of catharsis.

—DOROTHY PARKER (1893–1967), AMERICAN AUTHOR

Books are the quietest and most constant of friends; they are the most accessible and wisest of counselors, and the most patient of teachers.

—CHARLES W. ELIOT, *THE HAPPY LIFE* (1896)

When you are at the end of your rope, tie a knot and hang on!

—FRANKLIN D. ROOSEVELT (1882–1945), THIRTY-SECOND PRESIDENT OF THE UNITED STATES

To be what we are,
And to become what we are capable of becoming,
Is the only end to life.

—ROBERT LOUIS STEVENSON (1850–1894),
SCOTTISH NOVELIST, ESSAYIST, AND POET

To me the sole hope of human salvation lies in teaching.

—GEORGE BERNARD SHAW (1856–1950), BRITISH DRAMATIST,
PAMPHLETEER, AND CRITIC OF MUSIC, THEATER, AND SOCIETY

Getters generally don't get happiness; givers get it. You simply give to others a bit of yourself—a thoughtful act, a helpful idea, a word of appreciation, a lift over a rough spot, a sense of understanding, a timely suggestion. You take something out of your mind, garnish in kindness out of your heart, and put it into the other fellow's mind and heart.

—GERALD HESSE (1901–1969), AMERICAN PHILANTHROPIST

When the going gets tough, when the kids are not directing their energies on our subject, I pull out a good book and read out loud to them. Find a book that illustrates the problems we're having. Either way, it redirects our attention and usually casts a favorable light on things. If the day goes badly and I need to get away from those feelings, I often read for a while when I get home.

—PATRICIA BELL, THIRD- AND FOURTH-GRADE TEACHER,
FORT COLLINS, COLORADO

The love of learning, the sequestered nooks and all the sweet serenity of books.

—HENRY WADSWORTH LONGFELLOW (1807–1882),
MORITURI SALUTAMUS

How many a man has thrown up his hands at a time when a little more effort, a little more patience would have achieved success?

—ELBERT HUBBARD (1856–1915), AMERICAN AUTHOR,
MAGAZINE EDITOR, AND SOCIAL CRITIC

Teaching itself has been handicapped by spurious educational thinkers, endemic politicking, untalented recruits, professional organizations more interested in work rules than in student achievement, poor support from parents, and all the structural ills of a cancerous bureaucracy. If any problem could afflict American schools in theory, it probably does in fact.

—MARVIN CETRON AND OWEN DAVIES, *CRYSTAL GLOBE* (1991)

Humor must not professedly teach and it must not professedly preach, but it must do both if it would live forever.

—Mark Twain (1865–1910)

Humor is the shortest distance between two people.

— Henny Youngman (1902?–1998), American humorist

It's neat when you tell one good joke every now and then.

—Jeff J., fifth grade, Vernal, Utah

There was a kind lady called Gregory
Said: "Come to me, poets in beggary"
But found her impudence
When thousands of students
Cried: "All we are in that category."

—James Joyce, *Ulysses* (1922)

Little Sammy approached Papa in the evening with his schoolbooks. "Say, Pop," he asked, "will you help me with my 'rithmetic problems?"

"What are they about, son?" asked the father.

"Teacher say we gotta find the least common denominator," Sammy said.

"Good gosh," his father yelled in disgust. "Ain't they found that yet? They was a lookin' fer it when I was a boy."

—W. K. McNiell, editor, *Ozark Mountain Humor* (1989)

Put comics on the chalkboard to get them started on the day.

—KIM L., THIRD GRADE, FORT COLLINS, COLORADO

Humor is essential to any smoothly functioning system of interaction, to any healthy person, and to any viable group. Humor is, in the last analysis, no joke.

—GARY FINE, PROFESSOR OF EDUCATION, UNIVERSITY OF MINNESOTA

Good humor is one of the best articles of dress one can wear in society.

—WILLIAM MAKEPEACE THACKERAY (1811–1867)

Laughter's like a seedling,
Waiting patiently to sprout.
All it takes is just a push
To make it pop right out.

—DAVID SALTZMAN, AMERICAN AUTHOR
AND ILLUSTRATOR

A daily dose of humor goes a long way in my classroom. Teaching is both an art and a science. The science comes in planning and organizing. The art, well, that takes real "heart."

—DIANE LOOMANS, *THE LAUGHING CLASSROOM* (1993)

A day without laughter is a day wasted.
> —CHARLIE CHAPLIN (1889–1997), ENGLISH-BORN AMERICAN
> HUMORIST, SOCIAL CRITIC, AND FILM STAR

Don't wear the same shirt all year long. We can tell you wash it because the palm trees are fading.
> —JOSHUA A., SIXTH GRADE, CLEARWATER, FLORIDA

Always make the consequences of classroom discipline proportionate with the infraction. Nothing ruins order and respect more than discipline that doesn't fit the misbehavior.
> —SUE LAROY, PRESIDENT, IMAGININGS, INC. AND
> FORMER EDUCATOR, PORTLAND, OREGON

A gentle answer turns away wrath, but a harsh word stirs up anger.
> —PROVERBS 15:1

Praise in public; appraise in private.
> —KIPPER R., COLLEGE STUDENT, CHARLOTTE, NORTH CAROLINA

Achievement is largely the product of steadily raising one's levels of aspiration and expectation.
> —JACK NICKLAUS, *MY STORY* (1997)

If you judge people, you have no time to love them.

—MOTHER TERESA OF CALCUTTA (1910–1997),
YUGOSLAVIAN-BORN CATHOLIC MISSIONARY

Every day millions of students arrive at American class-rooms in search of more than reading and math skills. They are looking for a light in the darkness of their lives, a Good Samaritan who will stop and bandage a burned heart or ego.

—JIM TRELEASE, AUTHOR OF *THE READ-ALOUD HANDBOOK*

Modern governments support research on education and other social sciences for a variety of reasons . . . They under-stand that information from research can raise important new questions about policies, help program performance, and help control program activities; more cynically, they also understand that research results can be used to legitimate policies and vindicate choices—including choices to delay.

—M. TIMPANE, *EDUCATIONAL RESEARCH,*
METHODOLOGY, AND MEASUREMENT (1988)

At present government sees schools as a service to parents. They are not. They are a service to children and to no one else. If children have to be dragged to them by so-called "wel-fare officers" the schools are clearly failing those children. Instead of branding absentees with the title of "truant" (orig-inally a medieval French bandit!) schools ought to be asking why their clients don't want what they have to offer.

—CHRIS SHUTE, *COMPULSORY SCHOOL DISEASE* (1993)

Classroom teaching is the low-status work of education . . . Yet despite their lesser pay, harder work, and fewer privileges the teachers who educate each generation are as important as researchers in university or institutions.

—IRA SHOR, *EMPOWERING EDUCATION* (1992)

Teaching is both one of the hardest and one of the easiest jobs in the world, depending on how conscientiously it is done. It is also one of the noblest and most corrupt occupations—again, depending on how it is done. Because of the greater freedom of professors, compared to school teachers, the sweep of variations tends to be even greater in higher education . . . cheap popularity, ego trips, and ideological indoctrination are just some of the pitfalls of teaching.

—THOMAS SOWELL, *INSIDE AMERICAN EDUCATION* (1993)

Teaching has ruined more American novelists than drink.

—GORE VIDAL, *OUI* (1975)

Teaching is the royal road to learning.

—JESSAMYN WEST, *THE LIFE I REALLY LIVED* (1979)

Some teachers find that co-teaching a class can be helpful to them and the student.

With the inclusion of special needs students within the classroom teachers are faced with a variety of struggles.

Whether instructing young students or adults, co-teaching can be a solution to teaching in "tough times."

If everyone in a class achieves the desired cognitive level of learning then the instructor is effective. Different instructors may be required to attain different cognitive levels since not all educators are prepared to teach to every level for every topic.

—LT. COL. MIKE SCHAEFER, U.S. ARMY RESERVES,
COMMAND AND GENERAL STAFF COLLEGE TRAINING BATTALION

When the going gets tough in the classroom what gets me through is a solid background in honesty, fairness, reasoning, and meaning. I do not include truth in the above because there are many "truths." I have found that being objective in my dealings with people and my students and having sought meaning and understanding in my work and life, that this supports my actions and behaviors today.

—LORENZO GONZALES, HIGH SCHOOL SCIENCE TEACHER,
CUBA, NEW MEXICO

When you're in a rut see what others are doing that is different. Sometimes changing grade levels can lift you out. Don't become discouraged when things don't go as you plan. Keep your enthusiasm, but temper it with self-discipline and maturity. Realize some things just come with experience.

—ROSEMARY MCKNIGHT, THIRD-GRADE TEACHER,
HENDERSON, TENNESSEE

Take a course or take a sabbatical. Change the grade, subject, building, or district where you teach. If nothing along this line works, don't stay in the profession. Too much is at stake both for you and the students.

—RAYNA LEVINE, PH.D., INDEPENDENT EDUCATIONAL CONSULTANT,
FORMER PRINCIPAL, OMAHA, NEBRASKA

I've never been lost; but I was bewildered once for three days.

—DANIEL BOONE (1734–1820), AMERICAN FRONTIERSMAN

One is never lost . . . if the experience of reading, discussing, traveling is an inherently vital and educational one.

—THOMAS E. BARRON, "FROM THE CLASSROOMS OF STANFORD TO THE
ALLEYS OF AMSTERDAM," IN *TEACHERS AS MENTORS* (1996)

Everything on the earth has a purpose,
every disease an herb to cure it,
and every person a mission.

—CHRISTINE QUINTASKET, AKA MOURNING DOVE (1888–1936),
NATIVE AMERICAN NOVELIST

Knowing others is intelligence; knowing yourself is true wisdom.

Mastering others is strength, mastering yourself is true power.

—LAO-TZU (604–531 B.C.), CHINESE
PHILOSOPHER AND FOUNDER OF TAOISM

They are able because they think they are able.

—Virgil (70–19 b.c.), Greek writer and poet

The mind is not a vessel to be filled, but a fire to be kindled.

—Plutarch (?–120 a.d.), Greek-born Roman
historian, philosopher, and biographer

Self-confidence is the first requisite to great undertakings.

—Samuel Johnson (1709–1784), English novelist,
poet, philosopher, and lexicographer

Daring ideas are like chessmen moving forward;
They may be beaten, but they may start a winning game.

—Johann Wolfgang von Goethe (1749–1832),
German poet, dramatist, novelist, and scientist.

The happiness of a man in this life does not consist in the absence but in the mastery of his passions.

— Alfred Lord Tennyson (1809–1892),
English poet and writer

Let no man imagine that he has no influence. Whoever he may be, and wherever he may be placed, the man who thinks becomes a light and a power.

—Henry George (1839–1897), American economist

Man can alter his life by altering his thinking.

> —WILLIAM JAMES (1842–1910), AMERICAN
> PHILOSOPHER AND PSYCHOLOGIST

I believe that any man's life will be filled with constant and unexpected encouragement, if he makes up his mind to do his level best each day, and as nearly as possible reaching the high water mark of pure and useful living.

> —BOOKER T. WASHINGTON (1856–1915), FORMER
> SLAVE AND FOUNDER OF THE TUSKEGEE INSTITUTE

If you think you can do a thing or think you can't do anything, you're right.

> —HENRY FORD (1863–1947), AMERICAN INDUSTRIALIST

You cannot acquire experience by making experiments. You cannot create experience.
You must undergo it.

> —ALBERT CAMUS (1913–1960), FRENCH
> EXISTENTIALIST NOVELIST

A master can tell you what he expects of you. A teacher, though, awakens your own expectations.

> —PATRICIA NEAL (B. 1926), AMERICAN ACTRESS

Failure comes only when we forget our ideals and objectives and principles.

—JAWAHARLAL NEHRU, INDIAN PRIME MINISTER, 1947–1964

The best way to escape from your problem is to solve it.

—ROBERT ANTHONY EDEN (1897–1977),
FIRST EARL OF AVON, ENGLISH PRIME MINISTER

Imagination grows by exercise.

—W. SOMERSET MAUGHAM (1874–1965),
ENGLISH NOVELIST

Perhaps the most valuable result of all education is the ability to make yourself do the things you have to do, when it ought to be done, whether you like it or not.

This is the first lesson to be learned.

—THOMAS HENRY HUXLEY (1825–1895),
ENGLISH SCIENTIST AND AUTHOR

Before beginning a hunt, it is wise to ask someone what you are looking for before you begin looking for it.

—A. A. MILNE (1882–1956), ENGLISH AUTHOR
AND CREATOR OF THE WINNIE-THE-POOH SERIES

And when all else fails, a simple kind act, a service for someone else, can bring you out of the depths and give you new perspective.

Kindness in words creates confidence, kindness in thinking creates profoundness, kindness in giving creates love.

—Lao-Tzu (604–531 b.c.), Chinese
philosopher and founder of Taoism

No act of kindness, no matter how small, is ever wasted.

—Aesop (?–550 b.c.), Greek writer

Kindness is the language which the deaf can hear and the blind can see.

—Mark Twain (1865–1910)

You cannot do a kindness too soon, for you never know how soon it will be too late.

—Ralph Waldo Emerson (1803–1882)

CHAPTER 12

From One Teacher to Another

When Helen Keller was a baby she contracted scarlet fever, which left her blind and deaf. Thrust into a world of dark silence she struggled to make sense of her surroundings. By the time she was seven, she was a belligerent and unhappy child, frustrated by her inability to communicate clearly with her family and others. Her parents, seeking help for her, hired Anne Sullivan, a teacher, who herself had experienced blindness. Sullivan helped Keller navigate through a silent and dark existence, challenging her to learn to overcome her physical adversity. Although she spent years struggling to communicate with those around her, Helen Keller, with the encouragement and instruction from Anne Sullivan, became a writer, speaker, and inspiration to people around the world.

Sometimes the best advice for teachers are the simple words of encouragement or advice about practical matters. Keller, who became a teacher to millions, learned from her teacher, and used her for counsel. Like her, teachers can learn best from those with experience.

The object of education is to prepare the young to educate themselves throughout their lives.

—ROBERT MAYNARD HUTCHINS, PRESIDENT OF
THE UNIVERSITY OF CHICAGO, 1945–1951

Whoever can see through all fear will always be safe.

—LAO-TZU (604–531 B.C.), CHINESE
PHILOSOPHER AND FOUNDER OF TAOISM

You are teaching a teacher.

—TITUS MACCIUS, AKA PLAUTUS (254–184 B.C.),
ROMAN SOLDIER, MERCHANT, AND MINSTREL

Why "liberal studies" are so called is obvious; it is because they are the ones considered worthy of free men. But there is really only one liberal study that deserves that name—because it makes a person free—and that is the pursuit of wisdom.

—LUCIUS ANNAEUS, AKA SENECA (4 B.C.–65 A.D.),
ROMAN DRAMATIST, PHILOSOPHER, AND STATESMAN

We can teach them but we cannot "learn" them.

—DR. CHARLES R. MCNERNEY, PROFESSOR OF MATHEMATICS,
UNIVERSITY OF NORTHERN COLORADO AT GREELEY

A teacher should give his pupil opportunity for independent practice without suggestions from himself, and thus, set upon him the stamp of indelible memory in its purest form.

—PHILO, AKA PHILO JUDAEUS OF ALEXANDRIA
(20 B.C.–50 A.D.), ROMAN THEOLOGIAN

Fads go through our society with great regularity. Educators, as part of society, are not immune to fads. We can chuckle at our students' search for the universal answer, and then we fall for the next and newest complete answer to the ills of education.

—WILLIAM E. HOFFMAN, D.D.S., M.S.D., CLINICAL PROFESSOR,
UNIVERSITY OF MISSOURI–KANSAS CITY

Nothing is so serious as treating serious subjects in a trivial manner, and similarly, nothing is more entertaining than treating trivialities in such a way that you make it clear you are doing anything but trifle with them.

—DESIDERIUS ERASMUS, *IN PRAISE OF FOLLY* (1509)

That which is static and repetitive is boring. That which is dynamic and random is confusing. In between lies art.

—JOHN LOCKE (1632–1704),
ENGLISH POLITICAL PHILOSOPHER

To be able to practice five things everywhere under heaven constitutes perfect virtue . . . [They are] gravity, generosity of soul, sincerity, earnestness, and kindness.

—CONFUCIUS (K'UNG FU-TZU) (551–479 B.C.)

Gratitude is not only the greatest of virtues, but the parent of all the others.

—MARCUS TULLIUS CICERO (106–43 B.C.),
ROMAN ORATOR AND STATESMAN

The first thing I try to do to start a class period is to take the subject we will be discussing and form a personal question about it. Give students time to reflect on it and then have one or two read their thoughts. At that point I try to take it back to an historical perspective. Giving students a chance to take the subject in a different direction is sometimes the most enjoyable part of teaching. Enabling students to express themselves can often make my day.

—BILL HECTOR, U.S. HISTORY TEACHER,
DOWNERS GROVE, ILLINOIS; RECIPIENT OF
THE MILKEN NATIONAL EDUCATOR AWARD

A true teacher defends his pupils against his own influence.

—AMOS BRONSON ALCOTT (1799–1888),
ORPHIC SAYINGS

All sober inquirers after truth, ancient and modern, pagan and Christian, have declared that the happiness of man, as well as his dignity, consists in virtue. Confucius, Zoroaster, Socrates, Mahomet, not to mention authorities really sacred, have agreed to this.

—JOHN ADAMS, SECOND PRESIDENT OF THE
UNITED STATES, IN *A DISSERTATION ON
THE CANON AND FEUDAL LAW* (1765)

Wisdom and knowledge, as a rule, as well as virtue, diffused generally among the body of the people, being necessary for preservation of their rights and liberties, and these depend on spreading the opportunities and advantages of education in the various parts of the country among the different people, it shall be the duty of the legislators and magistrates in all future periods of this commonwealth to cherish the interest of literature and sciences and all the seminaries of them—especially the University at Cambridge, public schools, and grammar schools in the towns.

—CONSTITUTION OF THE COMMONWEALTH OF MASSACHUSETTS,
CHAPTER V (VI), SECTION III, "THE ENCOURAGEMENT
OF LITERATURE, ETC." (1779)

Intellect may enslave us, if we are predisposed to like it; but intellect cannot warm us, or inspire us with passion.

—JOHANN WOLFGANG VON GOETHE (1749–1832),
GERMAN POET, DRAMATIST, NOVELIST, AND SCIENTIST

The day school of that time was respectable, and the boy had nothing to complain of. He hated it because he was here with a crown of other boys and compelled to learn by memory a quantity of things that did not amuse him.

—HENRY ADAMS, *THE EDUCATION OF HENRY ADAMS* (1905)

Self is the sole subject we study and learn . . . I bring myself to sea, to Malta, to Italy, to find new affinities between myself and my fellowmen, to observe narrowly the affections, weaknesses, surprises, hopes, doubts, which new sides of panorama shall call forth to me.

—RALPH WALDO EMERSON (1803–1882)

On many occasions I start my own personal "pity party." No one could possibly have it as bad as I do today! I have found a surefire way to get me out of that mode. When I have a few spare minutes (if you don't—create some!), I drift down to where our wonderful teacher who works with our severely mentally and/or physically disabled children has her class. To see what those children go through every minute of every day of the rest of their life certainly puts my "pity party" in perspective. It is a rarity that, even though life has dealt them a pretty poor hand, they are not smiling, full of joy, and usually wanting to hug. That usually ends my "pity party."

—STEVE WOOLF, PRINCIPAL, TONGANOXIE, KANSAS;
MIDDLE SCHOOL PRINCIPAL OF THE YEAR; RECIPIENT
OF THE MILKEN NATIONAL EDUCATOR AWARD

I soon astonished myself with the ease with which I made the letter and the thought was soon present, "If I can make four letters, I can make more . . . " With play mates for my teachers and pavements for my copy books, and chalk for my pen and ink, I learned to write.

—FREDERICK DOUGLASS, *THE LIFE AND TIMES OF FREDERICK DOUGLASS* (1881)

The best teachers teach their students to learn and love what they teach. You can tell because they have such a good time at it.

—GRACE H., TENTH GRADE, MOVILLE, IOWA

After I got so I could read a little, I used to take a great deal of satisfaction in the lives of men who had risen by their own efforts from poverty to success. It is a great thing for a boy to be able to read books of that kind. It not only inspires him with the desire to do something and make something of his life, but it teaches him that success depends upon his ability to do something useful. To perform some kind of service the world wants.

—BOOKER T. WASHINGTON, *MY LARGER EDUCATION* (1911)

I've found that when I work hard each semester to teach reporting and editing I'm rewarded first with good work by the end of the course and ultimately with cards, notes, and e-mails from students working as interns and graduates working in newspapers.

If I could collect money for every epiphany experienced by former students, I'd need no retirement fund. The greater treasure, though, is that the patience the students teach me helps me to nurture their development and wait for them to understand how classroom exercises and news stories written and edited lead to success on the job. I am also steadily amazed by the students who I thought paid no attention, yet absorbed so much. I guess I'm also humbled by that, because I've learned that I have to mind what I say because it could come back to me in the form of what students have adopted as words to live by. My politics stay out of the classroom. My ethics, my sense of fairness, and my quest for accuracy follow me into the classroom each day.

I want to be as good as those who taught me and produce better newsroom professionals.

Teaching is an awesome responsibility. I'm glad that I've been given the privilege to teach at the University of Arkansas. In so many ways, I'm becoming like my students. I've thought of my five years in the classroom, and now I "get it."

—GERALD B. JORDAN, ASSOCIATE PROFESSOR,
WALTER J. LEMKE DEPARTMENT OF JOURNALISM
AT THE UNIVERSITY OF ARKANSAS

Teaching is more difficult than learning because what teaching calls for is this: to let learn. The real teacher, in fact, let nothing else be learned than learning. His conduct, therefore, often produces the impression that we properly learn nothing from him, if by "learning" we now suddenly understand merely the procurement of useful information.

—MARTIN HEIDEGGER (1889–1976), GERMAN PHILOSOPHER

Anyone who stops learning is old, whether at twenty or eighty. Anyone who keeps learning stays young. The greatest thing in life is to keep your mind young.

—HENRY FORD (1863–1947), AMERICAN INDUSTRIALIST

School is the outcome for so many things. Health care issues, learning issues, emotional issues, social interaction, parenting practices—everything converges on the way children are functioning in school. And the outcome a student has depends, to a great extent, on how optimistic or pessimistic a teacher is regarding a specific child.

—MEL LEVINE, RHODES SCHOLAR AND PROFESSOR OF PEDIATRIC MEDICINE, UNIVERSITY OF NORTH CAROLINA, CHAPEL HILL; C. ANDERSON ALDRICH AWARD WINNER

There is no meaning to life except the meaning man gives to his life by the unfolding of his powers.

—ERICH FROMM (1900–1980), AMERICAN PHILOSOPHER AND AUTHOR

Sometimes when we are so busy acting like competent adults we forget just how hard it was for us to get where we are. We forget about the journey we've taken and the mistakes we've made that made the journey interesting. Maybe we should let our own guard down just a bit so that a child in need of special encouragement can get a peek at our own learning process and can then see that there are many ways to get where you want to go. It's a fun trip.

—ELIZABETH J. GRAHAM, LCPC, NCC,
OVERLAND PARK, KANSAS

Hope is both the earliest and the most indispensable virtue inherent in the state of being alive. If life is to be sustained hope must remain, even where confidence is wounded, trust impaired.

—ERIK ERIKSON, GERMAN PSYCHOANALYST AND
AUTHOR, IN *CHILDHOOD AND SOCIETY* (1950)

Experience is true to any person when he is himself alone . . . in true experience every expression is creative, the creation of a person one is and is becoming. There is only the exploration, spontaneously expressing, finding satisfaction in personal being.

—CLARK MOUSTAKAS,
THE AUTHENTIC TEACHER (1966)

The classroom is your domain and you are its leader. To be a successful leader, you must be in control. To be in control, you must earn the respect of your students. Forget about making them like you at the beginning, for that will come if you have their respect. You earn that respect by being fair and consistent in your treatment of each student. Never threaten. Establish goals for yourself and for your class and reexamine them often. Remember that each child is as special as he or she is different. Each student has something that he or she can do better than anyone else. Discover it and proclaim it. And don't forget, I'm always here to listen and to talk.

—JOSEPH R. LEBLANC, RETIRED K–12 ADMINISTRATOR,
TEACHER, AND COACH, KANSAS CITY, MISSOURI

My motivation in teaching came from my excitement about life. There is so much to be learned, to be discovered about ourselves and the world around us—it's all good. I taught English—composition and grammar, mostly—but that was just a front. I saw myself as a facilitator in the dance of learning because no subject is taught in a vacuum. English studies pull from sociology, science, psychology; physics touches on religion; mathematics overlaps with music. I told my students, "If you don't wake up every morning and have your mind blown by the way that everything interrelates, maybe you're not paying attention."

—CHRISTI CLEMONS HOFFMAN, ENGLISH TEACHER,
FORMERLY OF ECOLE ZARADI, GENEVA, SWITZERLAND

The instruction in the academic fields should be exclusively in the hands of the subject matter departments. Professors of educations should be statesmen in a profession.

—JAMES B. CONANT, *MY SEVERAL LIVES: MEMOIRS OF A SOCIAL INVENTOR* (1970)

The basic meaning of liberal education lies in its capacity to deliver man from that which binds him to set him free.

—MICHIO NAGAI, *HIGHER EDUCATION IN JAPAN* (1971)

The education profession is producing a vast number of people who want to live significant, important lives but lack the ability to satisfy this craving for importance by individual achievement. The country is being swamped with nobodies who want to be somebodies.

—ERIC HOFFER, LONGSHOREMAN AND SELF-EDUCATED PHILOSOPHER, *WALL STREET JOURNAL* (1978)

The gap between laymen and academic specialists constantly grows. I do not think the gap is attributable to the speed with which the frontiers of knowledge are pushed back; instead, it reflects the desire by academics to be thought part of a special, elite, intellectually rigorous world and fear that, if what we wrote is intelligible, the claim would be more easily dismissed.

—JULIUS GETMAN, *IN THE COMPANY OF SCHOLARS* (1992)

A liberal education is the heart of society, and at the heart of a liberal education is the act of teaching.

—A. BARTLETT GIAMATTI, *HARPERS* (1988)

We have definite preferences and our preferences make us unique.

—DR. WILLIAM FOX AND WILLIS BANKS, *NATIVE AMERICAN AND ANGLO BRAIN PROCESS PREFERENCES: DIFFERENCES AND SIMILARITIES* (1984)

How do you stay on the ball as a teacher every day? It's not hard. I'm constantly doing different things. I think the worst thing would be to become set in what I taught and do the same thing over and over. Since the students are often doing projects and building their own knowledge, I learn also, and things are always changing. It's never boring.

—FRANCES MCLEAN COLEMAN, HIGH SCHOOL SCIENCE TEACHER, ACKERMAN, MISSISSIPPI; ALBERT EINSTEIN DISTINGUISHED EDUCATOR FELLOW, MILKEN NATIONAL EDUCATOR AWARD WINNER

One word: Organization! The minute you stop to get organized during the teaching day you've lost your class. I have found that the more organized I am the better my day will be. I also make it a point to be at my classroom door every morning and greet each of my students with a very cheerful hello and hug. I can really get a handle on how each child is with that simple good morning greeting . . .

When a lesson has not gone as planned I try to get through it, but realize that it is not the end of the world. I can re-teach the objective tomorrow by trying another strategy.

When I need to start over I pick out an activity that I know my students enjoy and stop trying to fix the problems that have occurred in the earlier lesson. If the bad day has occurred because of behavior problems, I start over by removing the problem.

—MARY RANSONE, RETIRED SECOND-GRADE TEACHER,
MEMPHIS, TENNESSEE

The elementary school that functions effectively sends each child on to the next school with favorable attitudes toward both self and the school. This is primarily a matter of helping him feel that he is acceptable and adequate. Identifying and providing experiences that will develop this security is a matter of guidance.

—MARIAN L. CARROLL, "EFFECTIVE GUIDANCE OF THE
ELEMENTARY SCHOOL CHILD," IN *INCREASING THE
HOLDING POWER OF THE CLASSROOM* (1966)

School phobia—Some children develop such a phobia about school and, far from malingering or needing a firm hand, may get into such a state of fear and panic about school that their enforced presence there may become impossible. What often puzzles teachers of these children is that before such an outburst the child may have been working quite well at school or even enjoyed it.

—*PRENTICE-HALL ENCYCLOPEDIA OF EDUCATION* (1970)

Educational reform must start with how students learn and how teachers teach, not with legislated outcomes.

—JACQUELINE GRENNON BROOKS AND MARTIN G. BROOKS,
*IN SEARCH OF UNDERSTANDING: THE CASE FOR
CONSTRUCTIVIST CLASSROOMS* (1999)

Let the wise listen and assist to their learning, and let the discerning get guidance.

—PROVERBS 1:5

I not only set high expectations for individual students, I hold myself to high standards as well. If success comes, it does so because I try to be consistent in what I say and follow through on consequences. I try to get parents active and try to be a role model myself. If I fail in anything, the kids notice . . . a lot! I do make an effort to admit my mistakes.

—MELINDA ABITZ, FIFTH-GRADE TEACHER,
TOPEKA, KANSAS

The rate of change is, if anything, increasing; therefore, adapting to change must be the center of any new kind of teaching.

—ROBERT ORNSTEIN AND PAUL EHRLICH,
NEW WORLD NEW MIND (1989)

Students are inherently curious about life and what is around them. They respond well to the joy of knowing more about things that interest them. Achieving is a great reward in itself—it feels good. The intrinsic rewards of learning aren't always enough. It's okay to use praise, certificates, special privileges, small symbolic "gifts" to reward good effort and appropriate conduct . . .

Self-esteem comes not only from accomplishments but from the sheer act of trying to accomplish. It's the special feeling one finds when they do something they'd rather not do, but do anyway.

—DON WILSON, DIRECTOR OF OPERATIONS AND TRAINING,
THE TEEL INSTITUTE, KANSAS CITY, MISSOURI

Miss McMillen was my second-grade teacher. When I was in her class she was very loving and kind to me. She was also a very good teacher because she was so patient. Now, two years later, she still is very important to me because more than the ABCs she continually teaches me so much about important things such as kindness and goodness to other people.

Miss McMillen always stops and talks to me when we see each other, no matter how busy she is. She is always smiling and showing attention to all the students. Her kindness has taught me to treat other people with care. When someone is angry or unhappy, I think "why is the other person acting unkindly?" so I don't get upset. She has shown me how much fun it is to learn. How to do the best I can, to reach a little higher and not to be upset if I miss a goal, but to try again. Miss McMillen treats each kid like someone special. This year she is my brother's teacher. He loves her too and loves to go to school.

—Taylor Lamping, fourth grade,
Overland Park, Kansas

Teacher: Children, did you know that it is possible to play the piano by ear?

Fresh kid: So what? My grandfather is always fiddling with his whiskers.

—W. K. McNiell, editor,
Ozark Mountain Humor (1989)

CHAPTER 13

The Necessity of You, the Teacher

Thou shalt teach them diligently unto the children.

—DEUTERONOMY 6:7

Although often burdened with society's woes, blamed for the shortcomings of a school district, criticized for problems that come from low budgets and top-heavy administrations, teachers have the most important work. No surgeon would heal, no architect would build, no scientist would research without all the teachers that lead to those careers and many others. You only have to think of an elementary school lacking the third grade, a high school without the senior year, or a university without freshmen to realize the importance of your place in what could be called the Republic of Knowledge.

The necessity of you, the teacher, is fundamental. It can be abused or used to achieve greatness for your students, for you through your students' successes, and for the good of humanity as a whole. This is no less true today than it was in antiquity. Your job is noble, your mission divine.

I am not a teacher, but an awakener.

—ROBERT FROST (1874–1956), AMERICAN POET
AND FOUR-TIME WINNER OF THE PULITZER PRIZE

The authority of those who teach is often an obstacle to those who wish to learn.

—MARCUS TULLIUS CICERO (106–43 B.C.),
ROMAN ORATOR AND STATESMAN

Those who are enamored of practice without science are like a pilot who goes into a ship without a rudder or compass and never has any certainty where he is going.

—LEONARDO DA VINCI (1452–1519),
ITALIAN ARTIST, ARCHITECT, AND SCIENTIST

Every tiny step forward in the world was formerly made at the cost of mental and physical torture.

—FRIEDRICH WILHELM NIETZSCHE (1844–1900),
GERMAN PHILOSOPHER, POET, AND CLASSICAL PHILOLOGIST

Action and faith enslave thought, both of them in order not to be inconvenienced by reflection, criticism, and doubt.

—HENRI FREDERIC AMIEL (1821–1881), JOURNAL INTIME
(THE PRIVATE JOURNAL OF HENRI FREDERIC AMIEL)

Education has for its object the formation of character. To curb restive propensities, to awaken dormant sentiments, to strengthen the perceptions, and cultivate the tastes, to encourage this feeling and repress that, so as finally to develop the child into a man of well proportioned and harmonious nature—this is alike the aim of parent and teacher.

—HERBERT SPENCER (1820–1903), BRITISH PHILOSOPHER

My experience and observation have taught me that people who try to withhold the best things in civilization from any group of people, or race of people, not infrequently aid that people to the very things that they are trying to withhold from them . . .

Once he gets the idea that—because he has crammed his head full with mere book knowledge—the world owes him a living, it is hard for him to change.

—BOOKER T. WASHINGTON,
MY LARGER EDUCATION (1911)

We have moved swiftly from a time when the main task was to hasten further the achievement of educational conditions consistent with the democratic aspiration to one in which the survival of the democratic spirit is our major concern.

—HENRY GORDON HULLFISH, *EDUCATIONAL FREEDOM IN AN AGE OF ANXIETY* (1953)

You see things; and you say, "Why?"

But I dream things that never were; and I say, "Why not?"

—GEORGE BERNARD SHAW (1856–1950)

Love of power is the chief danger of the educator, as of the politician; the man who can be trusted in education must care for his pupils on their own account, not merely as potential soldiers in an army of propagandists for a cause.

—BERTRAND RUSSELL (1872–1970), ENGLISH
MATHEMATICIAN, LOGICIAN, AND PHILOSOPHER

Cram them full of noncombustible data, chock them so damned full of "facts" they feel stuffed, but absolutely "brilliant" with information. Then they'll feel like they're thinking.

—RAY BRADBURY, *FAHRENHEIT 451* (1953)

The root origin of the word education is *educare*, which means to care for, nourish, cause to grow. To educate, then, does not mean merely to inject with knowledge but to help to master the process of investigating what knowledge is for.

—STEVE ALLEN (1921–2000), AMERICAN HUMORIST,
MUSICIAN, AND TELEVISION STAR

Too many students are very good at taking tests, while too few students are good at logical and holistic thinking. Business today needs creative people who can think logically and communicate clearly.

—DANIEL LEE, LEE & ASSOCIATES, ATLANTA, GEORGIA

Elementary education consisted mainly of the "three Rs," taught by private tutors who, early in the fourth century, were paid fifty denarii a month for each student—a poor wage.

—KEITH BRANIGAN, *ROMAN BRITAIN* (1980)

In the classic definition [a mentor] is, at its best, a close, intense, mutually beneficial relationship between someone who is older, wiser, more experienced, and more powerful with someone younger or less experienced. It is a complex relationship within an organizational or professional context, built on both the mentor's and the protégé's needs.

—JOAN JERUCHIM AND PAT SHAPIRO, *WOMEN, MENTORS, AND SUCCESS* (1985)

My own view is that a well-trained and effective teacher is still preferable to the most advanced technology, and that even excellent hardware and software are of little avail in the absence of appropriate curricula, pedagogy, and assessment.

—HOWARD GARDNER, *THE UNSCHOOLED MIND* (1993)

When someone is absent we get to help that person by helping them with their assignments.

JENNIFER S., SIXTH GRADE, HOLLAND, MICHIGAN

I like it when a student gets to be the teacher. You get to have a spelling bee or give math problems and it's fun because you get to do different things.

LEE B., SIXTH GRADE, PORTLAND, OREGON

Traditional teaching methods convince students that they are stupid and inferior because they can't do arithmetic, that they have no knowledge to share with others, and that they are cheating if they do their homework with others. Such methods effectively prepare students to compete for work at boring jobs over which they have no control.

—MARILYN FRANKENSTEIN, *CRITICAL MATHEMATICS EDUCATION* (1987)

Teachers will never be replaced by technology. However, teachers who use technology will replace those who don't . . . Good teachers will include technology as part of their professional development. Excellent teachers will encourage, inspire, mentor, and help their colleagues to do the same.

—SUSAN STUCKER, FOREIGN LANGUAGE TEACHER FOR GRADES NINE TO TWELVE, WINDOW ROCK, ARIZONA; RECIPIENT OF THE MILKEN NATIONAL EDUCATOR AWARD

As a high school teacher concerned with teaching my students research and communication skills in the life sciences, I have at times kept lists of scientific research questions that come to mind as I go about my various obligations. I have found that by involving myself in new or original situations or by learning new concepts, the formulation of new research questions is automatic.

The new situation becomes the seed crystal dropped into the supersaturated solution. The supersaturated solution then begins to form a network of crystals as the seed crystal enters it.

In other words, what I do is acquire new knowledge or learn new principles through new situations and experiences. These new situations and experiences become the catalyst that promotes the formulation of new research questions by associating previous knowledge with newly acquired knowledge or even making new associations from previous knowledge.

—LORENZO GONZALES, HIGH SCHOOL TEACHER,
CUBA, NEW MEXICO

The merchants have invaded the temple and turned it into a market of exchange, where things bought and sold are not only idols and consumer goods, but also human souls. All too often, the schools deemed to be "good" are those which are good for the economy, attracting industry, grant money, and droves of students.

—D. PATTERSON, *THE MAIN SCHOLAR:
A JOURNAL OF IDEAS AND PUBLIC AFFAIRS* (1991)

It is in and through education that a culture, and polity, not only tries to perpetuate but enacts the kind of thinking it welcomes, and discards and/or discredits the kinds it fears.

—ELIZABETH KAMARCK MINNICH,
TRANSFORMING KNOWLEDGE (1990)

Learning is the natural reward of meetings with remarkable ideas and remarkable people.

—DAVID BAYLES AND TED ORLAND,
ART AND FEAR (1993)

The Crow and the Pitcher
Aesop's Fables

A poor crow who was near to death with thirst suddenly saw beneath her a water pitcher. Relieved, with great joy she flew swiftly down to it. However, although the pitcher contained water, its level was so low that no matter how she swooped and strained she was unable to reach it. Thereupon she tried to overturn the pitcher, hoping at least to drink from its spilled contents; but alas, it was too heavy for her.

At length, looking around, she saw some pebbles nearby. Picking them up, one by one, she dropped them into the pitcher. Slowly, by degrees, the water crept up to the very brim and she was at last able to quench her thirst.

Moral: Necessity is the mother of invention.

A sense of accountability is fostered when students are given a reason to be proud when they accept their responsibilities, and a reason to be sorry when they do not.

—LESLIE DUNN, EXECUTIVE DIRECTOR OF THE TEEL
INSTITUTE FOR DEVELOPMENT OF INTEGRITY AND
ETHICAL BEHAVIOR, KANSAS CITY, MISSOURI

Teachers need to show trust and give students a chance to perform. A few may not make it but everyone will benefit from the experience. When I start a lesson I'm not always sure where the end will be, but I'm confident that my students will gain something from the experience.

I have found that I have become a better teacher by being willing to let my students have more opportunities to succeed. It brings out the best in all of us.

—BILL HECTOR, U.S. HISTORY TEACHER, DOWNERS GROVE,
ILLINOIS; RECIPIENT OF THE MILKEN NATIONAL EDUCATOR AWARD

Trying to instill responsibility without measuring success or failure is like not paying attention to the gas gauge on your car and hoping that the car will run forever. One aspect of learning responsibility is experiencing the consequences of being irresponsible. I'm not a proponent of pass/fail courses. The world simply doesn't work that way. Setting students out into the "real" world without teaching them the consequences of not being responsible is like sending sheep among wolves. Measurements have nothing to do with fairness and everything to do with what we experience in everyday life.

—ADAM CULTER, HIGH SCHOOL ENGLISH TEACHER,
PORTLAND, OREGON

The teacher's task is not to implant facts but to place the subject to be learned in front of the learner and, through sympathy, emotion, imagination, and patience, to awaken in the learner the restless drive for answers and insights which enlarge the personal life and give it meaning.

—NATHAN M. PUSEY, FORMER PRESIDENT OF
LAWRENCE COLLEGE AND HARVARD